BLACKS IN THE AMERICAN WEST

EDITORS

Richard Newman
Marcia Renée Sawyer

The involvement of blacks at every point in the exploration, history, and ongoing life of the American West remains a little-known story. The books—both fiction and nonfiction—in this series aim to preserve these stories and to celebrate the achievement and culture of early African American westerners.

Fugitive Slave in the Gold Rush

Life and Adventures of James Williams

James Williams

Introduction to the Bison Books Edition by
Malcolm J. Rohrbough

UNIVERSITY OF NEBRASKA PRESS
LINCOLN AND LONDON

⊗

First paperback printing: 2002
Library of Congress Cataloging-in-Publication Data
Williams, James, b. 1825.
[Life and adventures of James Williams]
Fugitive slave in the Gold Rush : life and adventures of James Williams /
James Williams ; introduction to the Bison Books edition by Malcolm J. Rohrbough.
p. cm.—(Blacks in the American West)
Previously published as: Life and adventures of James Williams. Philadelphia :
A.H. Sickler, 1893.
Includes index.
ISBN 0-8032-9812-9 (pbk. : alk. paper)
1. Williams, James, b. 1825. 2. Fugitive slaves—United States—Biography.
3. Underground railroad. 4. African American pioneers—California—Biography.
5. California—Gold discoveries. 6. Frontier and pioneer life—California.
7. California—Race relations.
I. Title. II. Series.
E450.W72 2002
973.7′115′092–dc21
[B]   2002071467

Contents

Introduction

Malcolm J. Rohrbough

With the emergence of the abolition movement in the 1830s came a growing number of first person accounts by African-American refugees from southern slavery. These records of the inhumanity of the slave system, which played an important role in demonizing slavery and in celebrating the Underground Railroad, appeared both in abolition newspapers and in pamphlet form. The best known of these accounts was the *Narrative of the Life of Frederick Douglass*, but there were many others. James Williams's *Life and Adventures* is one of the most intriguing.

Born a slave in Maryland, at the age of thirteen Williams crossed the line into Pennsylvania and freedom. He was one of many African Americans active in the Underground Railroad who assisted other slaves in their flight to freedom. Williams differed from others in one important respect, however, for he traveled to California to participate in the gold rush. Although he returned to the East Coast on occasion, after the gold rush Williams lived much of the remainder of his life in California. His account of the life of a free African American (that is, an escaped slave) in the gold fields is one of the few such accounts we have. His narrative is an important chronicle of a freed slave making his way in the chaos and confusion of the nation's greatest lottery for wealth.

The California that James Williams encountered on landing at San Francisco in May 1851 had already seen several cycles of immigration and economic change. James W. Marshall's discovery of gold nuggets in John Sutter's mill race on the American River on 28 January 1848 began what is known as the California gold rush. In its initial stages the search for gold led to the wholesale movement of population to areas that included urban and rural sites of northern and central California as well as locations along a series of streams flowing west out of the Sierra Nevada. This early mining began with the pan but soon moved to the rocker; both techniques were worked by individuals or small groups (although some early entrepreneurs employed gangs of Indian laborers to process the gravel of the water courses). This reliance on individuals and small groups continued through the year 1848, as prospective miners arrived from Oregon Country, from the Hawaiian Islands, and from Northern Mexico. Indeed, the Mexican miners who flocked to what eventually became known as the Southern Mines were the first skilled miners of the gold rush.

By the first months of 1849 the tide of immigration from the East Coast of the United States had set in. Immigrants came first by ship and then, at the end of the summer, as part of the first of the great annual overland migrations. By the end of 1849 immigrants to California included representatives from all over the world, including large numbers of Western Europeans, Australians, and Chinese (although the large Chinese migration did not begin until 1852). These massive movements of people are reflected in the number of miners living in the gold country: probably five thousand at the end of 1848, forty thousand at the close of 1849, fifty thousand at the end of 1850, and, by the end of the mining season of 1851, one hundred thousand miners.

From the initial reports that reached the East Coast in the fall of 1848 it is clear that the search for gold in California was viewed as a great economic opportunity. Indeed, it was the perfect example of economic democracy in America, where individuals without name, education, or capital could become rich. To an astonishing degree the original rumors were true. Gold was found in California in growing quantities: from an amount worth $250,000 in 1848, $10 million in 1849, and $41 million in 1850, to $75 million in 1851, the year of James Williams's arrival. Having this great number of miners crowded together gave rise to a sense of competition. And, as individuals and groups jostled in ever more confined spaces (in some cases reducing the size of a claim to ten feet square), so did the dominant numbers of American miners begin to discriminate against foreign miners or any group that was different. At first the target of discrimination was the large number of Mexicans, but the growing hostility eventually spread to include all non-English-speaking miners. The two institutions that were used to discriminate were the Foreign Miners Tax of 1851 (which imposed a tax of twenty dollars a month on all foreign miners) and the miner's districts that passed ordinances against foreign miners. In response to the new tax many Mexican miners left the mines; the main targets of the Foreign Miner's Tax then became the French, the Chileans, the Peruvians, and especially the Chinese.

James Williams left San Francisco and went upriver to Sacramento in May 1851 during the opening of the third mining season in gold country. He arrived at a time of increasing competition with an accompanying fall in wages (both of which were naturally tied to the opportunities in the mines), and he faced even more pervasive discrimination against outsiders. Larger mining enterprises, which consisted of groups of investors who brought together capital to build dams and mine riverbeds, had appeared in increasing numbers and there was growing interest in the possibility of underground quartz mining with its heavy investment, wage labor work force, and industrial processes. These new techniques for mining signaled a vast change from the original economic opportunities available to individuals and small groups.

By his own account James Williams landed at Sacramento in mid-May 1851 and immediately went to work at the mines. He mined first at a gold camp named "Negro Hills," a camp whose name reflected its original inhabitants like the three thousand or so other mining camps in the California gold country, that is, the first miners at the site were African Americans. Williams's observation that "I worked there some time and made nothing but my board" (22), reflects the realities of the third mining season. He soon left for Kelsey's Diggings. His comment that "I packed my rocker that we washed the gold with, my prospect-pan, and my pick and shovel, and led the way" (22) suggests that he worked with a group of miners. A mining company of five to eight men was the most efficient number for living and working in the region; a rocker needed at least four men for efficient operation. By the third season of mining in California a pick, a shovel, and a pan could help in locating a claim, but a rocker was the device through which the gravel of the claim was washed.

In his account Williams described the proceedings of a miner's court in the trial of a miner for theft. Almost from the beginning of systematic mining in California the miners came together to organize "mining districts" and to lay down the rules for conduct of those within the district. The main business of the district was to pass laws governing mining claims and the size and conditions under which those claims were held, vacated, or sold. Of equal importance were questions of domestic order, especially in remote mining camps where institutions of law permeated only gradually and even then were met with some resistance. Miners always had confidence in the democratic structure of the mining district, a structure under which those gathered could claim sovereignty and pass regulations on a wide range of local issues. Because of the close conditions associated with working and living at the mines, the question of theft was always a pressing one (especially since miners worked the claims during the day, which left their living quarters deserted in their absence). Miners hated camp thieves and enforced severe penalties on those found guilty of stealing from their fellow miners. At the same time, the judicial proceedings to establish innocence or guilt were quick and informal. A jury was chosen, the parties stated their case to the miners assembled, and the jury delivered a verdict. The sentence that followed a guilty verdict was immediately carried out. Miners had a low opinion of formal law and lawyers, whom they regarded as engaged in collusion to charge fees for services or to raise technicalities under which guilty parties might sometimes go free.

Furthermore, mining camps had no jails and had no wish to bear the cost of incarceration. Court proceedings were designed to reach a verdict quickly and cheaply. In the case that Williams analyzed, the miners' court used the threat of violence to force the accused miner to give up the money. Once the money was returned the guilty party was probably expelled from the camp. Williams noted, "I was the only colored man in the crowd, and it was left for me to pass my opinion, and I said, 'If he gives up the money let him go'" (23). That he was the only African American in the crowd was not remarkable, but it probably was unusual that the crowd had asked his opinion. He later observed that by the time of his return to San Francisco in the fall of 1853, "the state of things is much better now in California than was the case on my arrival there" (23). In regards to the formal institutions of law and a court system, Williams was undoubtedly correct. At the same time, however, the white men who ran these new institutions were probably much less likely to ask the opinion of an African-American miner about any aspect of a criminal trial, unless he was the defendant.

Williams left Kelsey's Diggings to work in Sacramento, where he carried "the hod" for three months at six dollars a day. By the fall of 1851 the daily wage (which was always tied to returns from the mines) had fallen from twenty dollars a day in 1848 to a mere six to eight dollars a day. Williams's subsequent work experiences in California between 1853 and 1856—including owning a restaurant, as a laborer on the levee in San Francisco, as a wage laborer in the Southern Mines, owning a junk store in Sacramento, and driving an express wagon—was a cross section of the economic opportunities associated with the gold rush in the middle 1850s. That Williams owned a restaurant and a junk shop is testimony both to his enterprise and to the latitude available to African-American men in California at the time.

In 1859 Williams left Sacramento when the "Washoe excitement broke out" (28). His adventures on the Comstock Lode reflected another Western mining experience. The rush to what became known as the Comstock Lode in the summer of 1859 led to the opening of some of the great silver mines in the world and enormous profits for a few fortune founders and shareholders, as well as the creation of a large town, Virginia City, at the center of this mining enterprise. Williams was among the earliest commercial arrivals, and he made a tidy profit in flour and produce. Although he had intended to purchase property and presumably open a commercial establishment in Virginia City, Williams was dissuaded by the widespread civil violence he encountered. Instead, he went to Carson City where he bought lots, which he later sold in 1863.

Like so many others involved in the Comstock Lode excitement of the early 1860s, Williams had little to say about the great Civil War then raging in the East, a conflict brought on by a variety of issues, among them certainly the institution of slavery from which he had escaped. With a small number of noteworthy exceptions, Americans in the mining camps of the West between 1860 and 1865 energetically pursued opportunities for wealth with few if any thoughts about the issue of the Union. Williams's observations remind us of the great distance that separated the two coasts of the continental nation, distances that later were closed by the construction of the transcontinental railroad. The railroad eventually proved to be a useful source of labor for Williams, and beginning in 1872 he was "foreman of the whitewashers" for the Central Pacific Railroad (46).

Throughout his adventures Williams interspersed his observations on some of the noteworthy events of the day with homilies about religion and education. He quoted generously from Scriptures and indicated how its guiding principles assumed great importance in the many trials and travails of his own life. He was victimized on many occasions—by employers who failed to pay his wages, by schemes that played on his good nature, by the institutions of law and the court system brought to bear on an African-American man. Yet throughout these many travails he attempted to combine Christian forbearance with an independence of thought and deed. In making a judgment about the thief in the gold camp, for example, he affirmed that he could never be party to taking another life (23). For all of Williams's Christian patience, however, he was not one to turn the other cheek. From the first pages of his account the reader understands that Williams fought for himself (especially as a fugitive), for other African Americans, and for principles in which he believed. He mentioned several physical scars from these encounters, and the protagonists range from white gangs to black bullies to white police officers.

Williams also wrote in several places about the importance of education. He noted that had he enjoyed the opportunities of an education as a young man, he might have a accomplished even more as an adult. In his discussion Williams quoted both Milton and Shakespeare, suggesting that he himself understood the standard literary references of the day. To those without the opportunities of a liberal education he offered his own credo: "Press on!" (34). In his own experience he noted that "I have been without money, and I have been cast out in a strange land amongst strangers, without means. I kept on; I stroke to keep my head above the current. I did so" (35). Williams noted the remarkable progress of what he calls "the colored people." Held in bondage for 250 years, they had only just been freed. Consider the strides they made in such a short period of time. "Think of it," he wrote. "The Anglo-Saxon race, had they been under the same yoke, would they this day be any better than we are?" The answer is a clear *no*. In his final summing up, Williams favored the route of education and he urged everyone to seize the opportunities afforded in that direction. But he understood that the chances of African Americans may be reduced ones. "This is a white man's government," he wrote. "'A colored man has no rights that a white man is bound to respect'" (36–37).

Finally, Williams developed another theme throughout his narrative, namely the inconsistent behavior of African Americans both under the yoke of slavery and later under the freedom of the Thirteenth and Fourteenth Amendments. Blacks betrayed other blacks; they cheated other blacks; they gave false testimony against other blacks. He noted, "In my humble belief, they [colored people] are the most treacherous people in the city of Sacramento, State of California, or any portion of the world I ever traveled" (50). He concluded with, "But be it known, that the Anglo-Saxon race were my best friends through it all" (52).

Williams's strong support of religion and several "Anglo-Saxons" who befriended and aided him enhanced the attraction of his writings for readers. He wrote a pamphlet that he intended for sale, and the number of testimonials interspersed with his adventures testify to the commercial nature of the document. At the same time, Williams's escape from slavery, his participation in the work of the Underground Railroad, and his early and continued participation in the California gold rush and the subsequent mining rushes make his account an important source for historians in several fields.

Preface

The Author, thinking an account of his life and experience would be of service to persons into whose hands it might fall, has, by the advice of some of his friends, come to the conclusion to narrate, as correctly as possible, things that he encountered and that came under his notice during a period of some forty-five years. He hopes, after a perusal of his first attempt, the reader will pardon him for any errors which may have been committed; and if I can only think that any good may have grown out of my Adventures, I shall then consider that I have commenced to answer the end I and all human beings were created for — having lived that the world may be bettered by me.

John Thomas Evans, (*formerly,*)
Now James Williams.

San Francisco, —— ——.

I, John Thomas, was born in Elkton, Cecil county, Maryland, April 1, A.D. 1825, in the house of my master, William Hollingsworth, being born a slave. I remained with him until I was thirteen years of age, when I took one of his blooded mares and made my escape. Whilst riding, I met a number of men one of whom said to me: "Little boy, where are you going?" "I am going to Mr. Cuche's Mill." "Who do you belong to?" "I belong to Mr. William Hollingsworth." I at the time had on two pairs of pants, with leather suspenders over my coat. A man asked me, "Why do you wear your suspenders over your coat?" "These are my overalls, to keep my pants clean." Ere I arrived at Mr. Cuche's Mill I met a little boy. I said to him, "Little boy, what is the name of the next town beyond Mr. Cuche's Mill?" He told me, "New London Cross Roads." Ere I arrived there I met a white man. He accosted me thus: "Boy, who do you belong to?" I told him that I belonged to Mr. William Hollingsworth. "Where are you going to now?" "I am going to New London." At New London I met a school-boy. I asked him, "Where is the line that divides Maryland from Pennsylvania?" He said, "New London is the line?" I asked him, "What is the name of the next town?" He said, "Eaton Town." On my way I met another man; he said to me, "Where are you going?" I answered, "To Eaton Town." He said, "Where are you from?" I said, "Cuche's Mill." He asked me if I belonged to Mr. Cuche. I said, "Yes." On my way I met two more men.

They asked the same questions. I answered as before. When I arrived at Eaton Town, I asked a little boy what the name of the next town was. He said, "Russelville." As I went I saw a colored man cutting wood in the woods. I asked him, "What is the name of the next town?" He said, "Russelville." I asked him if any colored families lived there. He said, "Yes; Uncle Sammy Glasgow." He advised me to stop there. He asked me where I belonged. I said, "In New London Cross Roads;" and for fear that he would ask to whom I belonged, I whipped up my horse and went my way. I was then a few miles in Pennsylvania, and I felt that I was a free boy and in a free State. I met a man, and he asked me where I was going. I said, "Russelville, to Uncle Sammy Glasgow." He asked me if I was a free boy. I said, "Yes." He said, "You look more like one of those little runaway niggers than anything else that I know of." I said, "Well, if you think I am a runaway, you had better stop me, but I think you will soon let me go." I then went to Russelville, and asked for Sammy Glasgow, and a noble old gentleman came to the door, and I asked him if he could tell me the way to Somerset, and he pointed out the way. I asked him if he knew any colored families there. He said, "Yes." He told me of one William Jourden, the first house that I came to, on my left hand. This Jourden was my stepfather; he married my mother, who had run away years before, and the way that I knew where she lived was through a man by the name of Jim Ham, who was driving a team in Lancaster City, whose home was in Elkton. He came home on a visit, and was talking to one of the slave women one night; he sat with his arm around her, I, a little boy, sitting in the chimney-corner, asleep, as they thought, but with one eye open, and a listening. He whispered to her, saying, "I saw that boy's mother." She said, "Did you? Where?" He said, "In Somerset; she is married and doing well; she married a man by the name of William Jourden." When I arrived at my mother's house, I met my stepfather in the yard, cutting wood, and I asked him if Mrs. Jourden was at home. He said, "Yes," and asked me in. I went in and sat down by the door. My mother asked me my name. I answered, "James Williams." She said, "Come to the fire and warm yourself." I said, "No, that I was not cold." After sitting there awhile, I asked her if she had any children. She said, "Yes," and named one boy that belonged to William Hollingsworth, in Elkton.

I asked if she had any more. She named my sister, that belonged to
Thomas Moore, of Elkton, Vic, that had run away and was betrayed
by a colored man, for the sum of one hundred dollars. I had a brother
that went with my mother when she run away from Maryland. She did
not say anything about him, but spoke of John Thomas. I asked her if
she would know him if she saw him. She said, "Yes." I said, "Are you
sure that you would know him?" She answered, "Yes; don't you think I
would know my own child?" And becoming somewhat excited, she told
me that I had a great deal of impudence, and her loud tone brought her
husband in, and he suspicioned me of being a spy for the kidnappers.
He came with a stick and stood by the door, when an old lady, by the
name of Hannah Brown, exclaimed, "Aunt Abby, don't you know your
own child? Bless God, that is him." Then my mother came and greeted
me, and my father also. My mother cried, "My God, my son, what
are you doing here?" I said, that "I had given leg-bail for security." My
father took the horse and hid it in the fodder-stack. That night one
William Smith, who was a good old minister, went back on the road,
about six miles, with the horse, and put her on the straight road, and
started her for home; but the bridle he cut up and threw into a mill-race.
I was told that on the morning of the second day the horse stood at her
master's gate. To show the reader how my mother got free, I shall have
to digress a little. She was sold by Tom Moore to Mr. Hollingsworth,
for a term of two years, for the sum of one hundred dollars, and, at
the expiration of that time, she was to go back to Tom Moore's. One
morning Mr. Hollingsworth said, "Abby, it is hard enough to serve two
masters, and worse to serve three. You have got three months to serve
me yet, but here is twenty-five dollars. I won't tell you to run away.
You can do as you like." He told my uncle Frisby to take the horse and
cart and carry her as far as a brook, called Dogwood Run, on the way
to Pennsylvania. By these means my mother got her freedom, which
shows that Hollingsworth had a Christian spirit, though a slaveholder.
I stayed one night at my mother's, and in the morning I was taken on
the Underground Railroad, and they carried me to one Asa Walton,
who lived at Penningtonville, Pennsylvania, and he took me on one
of his fastest horses and carried me to one Daniel Givens, a good old
abolitionist, who lived near Lancaster City; and I traveled onward, from

one to another, on the Underground Railroad, until I got to a place of refuge. This way of travel was called the Underground Railroad. At the age of sixteen I commenced my labors with the Underground Road. The way that we used to conduct the business was this: A white man would carry a certain number of slaves for a certain amount, and if they did not all have money, then those that had had to raise the sum that was required. We used to communicate with each other in this wise: One of us would go to the slaves and find out how many wanted to go, and then we would inform the party who was to take them, and some favorable night they would meet us out in the woods; we would then blow a whistle, and the man in waiting would answer, "All right;" he would then take his load and travel by night, until he got into a free State. Then I have taken a covered wagon, with as many as fourteen in, and if I met any one that asked me where I was going, I told them that I was going to market. I became so daring that I went within twenty miles of Elkton. At one time the kidnappers were within one mile of me; I turned the corner of a house and went into some bushes, and that was the last they saw of me. The way we abolitionists had of doing our business was called the Underground Railroad; and in all my travels I always found the Anglo-Saxons to be my best friends.

The interpretation of the crowing of a chicken when Christ told Peter that he should deny him thrice before the cock crew: Peter denied him, and immediately the cock crew, and Peter immediately understood the interpretation. And that is the right interpretation which I have heard in the watches of the night, when I have been traveling with some fellow being towards the North Star and a land of freedom.

"Oh, give thanks unto the Lord God, for He is good, and His mercy endureth forever; He taketh my part against them that hate me. Oh, give thanks unto the Lord, for His mercy endureth forever.

When I was ten years old I was a house-boy. I had to stand at the table and brush off the flies while the guests were dining. General Sue, Col. Partridge and others would be in conversation and talking about the slaves, saying, "My negro Dick and my boy Tom," and discussing what they could get for their slaves; saying, that Bennet had captured his negro Bill, that run away two years ago, and is now in jail, and that he was the first well-dressed negro he met in Lombard street, Philadelphia, and when he recognized him, he said that he would come with him, and that he had no trouble to get him. One of the men turned his head, and said, "Tom, you must never run away. Bad boys are the only ones that run away, and when their master gets them, he will sell them to go to Georgia, where they will bore holes in your ears and plow you like a horse." Saying this for the purpose of frightening me, thinking that I would believe such stories. Seeing the difference between freedom and slavery, I made up my mind that when I was old enough I would run away. The reason I run away when I did was, because an old colored lady, by the name of Rachel, who was considered to be a good old aunty, became affronted at me, and misrepresented me, and told a lie on me, for which I was whipped with a rawhide very severely. Perhaps ere this she hath gone to eternity; if so, I hope ere she went she sought forgiveness, and is now resting from her labors, and the good works consummated by her are following her. Slaves, at times, did things which worked directly against each other, ignorantly. Be this as it may, the Creator hath a record of all transactions, and will, He says, render justice to all. I, therefore, leave the event to Him for adjustment. My master, in conclusion, threatened to sell me to Georgia. After receiving the chastisement, I went off sniffling and crying. On the following Sunday morning I arose quite early and gave them leg-bail for security, and on one of his blooded mares I run away from him, or, in other words, she done the running and I on her back. I was then satisfied that I was getting out of the way of old John Thomas, instead of old Dan Tucker, as goes the old song, where I was then. The traders and slave-hunters went to my master and tried to get him to advertise me or employ them to hunt me, as the partridge upon the hill; but he, being very close, would not employ them, but the law compelled him to advertise me, or pay a fine. He had such great confidence in me that I would come back again, that he said, "Oh, the boy has gone on a spree, and will be home again in a few days." He offered a reward of two cents to apprehend me, and four cents to let me go scot-free, and ten dollars reward for the recovery of his black mare. But the spree that he thought I had gone on was never over until the year 1868. Arriving in Pennsylvania in the year A.D. 1838, I went to work for an abolitionist, by the name of Asa Walton. It was in the winter, and when the spring opened I went to work for one Mr. Dickerson, in the year 1839, at five dollars per month. In A.D. 1840 I went to work for a Mr. Clarkson Crozier, at six dollars per month. He was also an abolitionist, and in 1841 I was still in his employ. When I was sixteen years of age I made a hand at mowing. In 1842 I was still in that employ, and led the field, and was foreman of the farm, where I remained until 1843. In 1844 I worked for one Mr. Hudson until September of the same year, when, to my great surprise, the kidnappers came upon me. The reader will not be surprised when I inform him of the fact that that was the first intimation I ever had of a surprise party; for I was so much taken by surprise, that I went down into the bushes, and that was the last they saw of me. Thus the reader can aver that I surprised them also. In six months after I was again in the same place. In 1845 I went to a quarterly meeting that was being held in Wilmington, Delaware, at which I saw several white men I knew, who came from the place of my birth that I had run away from. They made sure they had me then, but I slipt through the crowd, ran in and through the church, out of the back door, and into the wagon that I had tied there in the bushes behind the hill, and made off to New Gardens, that being the last they saw of me. I then went to Reading, Pa., and I there came in contact with the Underground Railroad. This was in 1846, and in 1847 I was again in Somerset township, where the kidnappers first made me leave. I was that year again living with Clarkson Crozier, still engaged in the Underground Railroad business, having a large light four-horse wagon, with white cover over it. I then assumed the name James Williams. I would say to men who asked me, "Where are you going, Williams?" I would tell them I was going to Lancaster to market. At other times, when meeting them and they would ask me where I was going, I told them to Wilmington market. The wagon would be shut up tight to keep the rain and snow from spoiling the grain, and, at the same time, perhaps, I would have a load of slaves in there. I have carried as many as fourteen women and children at a load. The way we managed to get away slaves from the Southern States, we used to have runners there, and when any one wanted to get away, he would go to one of these runners and tell him he wanted to make his escape, and the runner would ask if he could raise a party of ten or fifteen. "If you can, you must raise a certain sum of money; and if all have not got money, some must pay for others, until the money is raised, and then meet me at a certain place, with the amount of money. And now here is a whistle I will give you; set your party against a certain night, and walk three miles from the place where you started, to a certain place, and when you get there, if there is nobody within sight, or nobody around but your own party, you blow your whistle three times, and when I answer, come direct to the answer." Now the reader may have some understanding how the Underground Railroad was conducted. In 1848 I was attacked by a party of kidnappers on the Lancaster Turnpike, and I had no weapons, only those God gave me, and, at that time, feeling myself to be much of a man, I used the weapons upon them pretty severely, and when I found myself getting out of breath, I jumped the fence and run through the cornfields, and went to a farmer's house, and told him what had happened to me. I gave him three dollars to take me to the cars that run to Philadelphia, and, by this means, I got clear of them. After arriving there, I went to work in a brickyard, for a gentleman named Davis. I remained there until after the riot, taking part with the citizens against the Killers. I then made my escape to Reading, Pa. I remained there a few days, and, for fear of danger, I made my escape to Pottsville. This was still in 1848, and there I went to work in the coal mines. In the latter part of this year I left there and returned back to Philadelphia. In the beginning of 1849, I went to work for Mr. George Pickeron, who kept a hay-yard on Germantown road. He was a lawyer, also; he made me seller for him, and I remained with him about six months. I was walking out one evening, and was attacked by a set of white rowdies, and I having his pistol in my possession, I fired upon them, and I was taken that same night to the watch house, and on the next morning, he being a lawyer, and going my security, he took my case in hand and cleared me, for the sum of twenty-five dollars.

In the month of September, three days after, there was a large riot between the colored people and the Killers. I was identified with a company of young men, calling themselves the Stringers, and was placed that night as captain of the company. I fired the first shot on the Moyamensing Killers. When the California House was set on fire, at the corner of Sixth and St. Mary's alley, I rushed up to try to put it out, and was shot in my right thigh with buckshot, and also received a blow over my left eye—the mark of which is there until this day. I made my escape as soon as possible, and went to a doctor's; but the doctor, after looking at me, said, "You are not hurt; go and try them again." I went, and fought harder than ever. The women tore up all the sidewalk, so that the men could get bricks and stones to fight with. At two o'clock in the morning the fighting ceased, but was renewed again at seven, and I was the first who fired on the Killers that day. An officer, calling himself by the name of Craig, attempted to arrest me, but I struck him a blow, which tumbled him to the ground. He got up and went away, but came back reinforced to arrest me, but the members of Goodwill Hose company, who were on the side of the colored citizens, came to my assistance, and then we had a free fight of it; but I am sorry to say there were seven or eight of that company shot that day. There were also two colored men shot, and several wounded, and the California House was burned to ashes. Cadwalader's company was called out to quell the riot, and succeeded in doing so. This riot was created by the Irish Democrats.

I then made my escape to New York, where I remained about three months, and then returned back to Philadelphia. A Mr. Morris Buckman gave me a schooner to run from there to New York. I took the schooner to Trenton, then crossed through the canal to New Brunswick, and from there we sailed to New York. She was consigned to his brother. We laid at the Pier No. 2, North River.

Early in 1850 I returned back to Philadelphia, and went into the ice-cream and fruit business. One night I went out to have a little fun at a swing-yard that was kept by a Mr. Dennis; got into company with a couple of ladies, and there came a Mr. Brown, weighing about 190 pounds, forbidding me keeping company with those ladies. We had a great deal of controversy about it, and at last we came to blows; but he was no more than an Indian rubber ball in my hands. After a few rounds the watchman sprung his rattle, and we all commenced running. I jumped a fence six feet high, out into an alley, in which happened to be living a family that I was acquainted with. Having lost my hat, I stood in their doorway bare-headed; the watchman came running by, looking for the man that jumped the fence, and he asked me if I had seen a man jump the fence. I told him yes, and that he had just run down the street. Away he run after him, as he thought, and I borrowed a hat, went home and got to bed. A few days after that a colored man was arrested as a fugitive from labor, a slave, and, as was always my lot, I was into that fight. I was one of the men that helped to guard the Court-House all night, and stood watch to prevent him from being stolen from the watch-house. I was also one of the men that formed the plan to tear up the Wilmington railroad track to keep them from getting him away. At last they succeeded in stealing him away from us. Thank God! slavery is dead now, and we will be troubled no more with that abominable curse, and I hope the time will come when we will be on a level with the Anglo-Saxon race, and the time not far distant when we will receive the full rights of American citizens. I thank God that I, who was once a slave, can lay down at night and take my rest without being afraid or molested, but can sleep with the consciousness that I am a freeman, and protected as such, and no longer looking towards the hills for refuge. But whom do I thank for it and whom do I praise, or in whom do I put my trust? In the great God of heaven and of earth; and since I have put my trust in Him I must also follow Him, and so long as I follow Him I will fear no evil. The God who delivered Daniel out of the den of lions is able to deliver me also; and He has delivered me and kept me until this time, and I praise Him and give Him thanks forever.

In the same year I saw a white man in Market street, whom I knew, and who thought he was smart enough to catch me, and seeing him, I crossed the street, and went into a store, and let on that I did not notice him. But, like a cat, I always slept with one eye open, and when I traveled I always kept a keen eye and listening ear, and a silent tongue upon everything that I thought would betray me, and I never let it be known to any one that I was a fugitive until this day. When I came out of the store I quickly noticed that this white man had sent a policeman to arrest me—this policeman going some distance below me, and standing on the corner, and the man standing above on the other corner. This being done, I was in the middle. I was looking over my shoulder, and saw him beckon and point his finger. I then crossed the street, as if I noticed nothing, and in quick time. I then looked over my shoulder a second time, and saw him crossing after me. I then turned up a little alley in double quick time, and turning up another alley I left them out of sight. I then went to my boarding-house, kept by Mr. Hargas, on Eleventh street, near Lombard, four doors from the Masonic Hall. Mrs. Hargas said to me: "Mr. Williams, there has been two white men here looking for you; they have just gone; they asked me if I knew where they could find you, and I told them no—I did not know—they looked like strangers to me; they went down Lombard street." I paid my bill, telling Mrs. Hargas that I was going to Lancaster City, she not knowing that I was a fugitive slave. I also said to her, "If they call again tell them that I am going to Lancaster city." I packed up my little trunk and went down South street in quick time, and meeting a colored man I gave him my trunk and told him to carry it down to the boat that went to New York. "Get me a check and say nothing to any one and bring it back to a certain corner to me." He did so. I then went very near to the boat landing to a certain alley, where were some sugar casks, and stowed myself away there, like a fox when the hounds are after him, and my heart appeared to be in my throat. I had never told anybody about the circumstances under which I was placed, and the danger which I was in; consequently I had no one to console me, or no friends to help rescue me, but, when the bell was ringing and I saw a chance to flee from danger, I ran and leaped aboard the boat, and was soon on my way to Trenton, but yet I felt a little alarmed. After landing there, I had to wait an hour for the down train, and still felt alarmed. During the time I was waiting, I did not know at what moment I might be arrested, and I looked upon every white man as my enemy at that time. Becoming hungry, I walked a short distance to a cake shop, ate a couple of pies, a few doughnuts, drank part of a bottle of spruce beer, put a few cakes into my pocket, and then asked the young man how much the bill was. He said forty cents, and I told him to charge it to Mr. Barnburner, and he said, "Yes, sir," and he went to the desk, took a pen and put it down in his book. I then said to him, "Did you charge it?" and he said, "Yes, sir," and he further said, "Thank you, sir—you must come again." By that time the cars had come, and I jumped aboard, and left that place as soon as I could, and felt released from danger. The next place I landed at was New York city. As soon as I landed at New York I went to work in a private boarding-house, kept by Mrs. Lent, on Leonard street and Broadway. After being there a few days, there was a colored man arrested at the Irving House, corner of Broadway and Chambers streets, by the name of Henry Long. I went down to engage in a fight for him, and stayed there until he was delivered up to those who claimed to be his masters; but I and another colored man attacked his master in the night time, in a public square, and he drew a six-shooter on us, and we gave back like cowards. We went next day to have him arrested, but as we made the attack on him first we did not succeed, so poor Henry was sent back. A few evenings after that I went to the Knickerbocker Saloon, on Church street, near Thomas, where there was a raffle, and I commenced throwing chances, and as luck would have it, won two of them. The company gathered there looked more like rowdies than any class of men that I could compare them to, and all strangers; but it being a raffle and the geese looked so fine and fat, I went in on that account and won them. One man says to me, "Old fellow, you have not won these geese fair! You shall put them up and raffle them again. You have thrown three sixes twice and you have fingered the dice; you must throw over again." Says I, "I shall not do it." "Well, if you don't, we will put a topnot over your eye." I, feeling myself pretty much of a man, said that I should carry the geese away with me, and that I could whip any man in the house, one after the other. A little boy, about twelve years of age, reminded me of a little fierce dog barking at a large dog by jumping out before me and saying, "You ——————— nigger, you can't whip me!" shaking his fist in my face. I picked up my geese and started out doors, telling them to stand back, but they surrounded me in the street, and while talking to them one fellow struck me over the eye and landed me half way across the street. Falling to the ground, my geese went one way and my plug hat another. When I received that blow I thought that I saw stars. I lay some seconds as a dead man, and when I arose I commenced calling out for the watchman, who came and rescued me. He went with me to pick up my hat and into the house where the affair happened to arrest the man that struck me and to get my geese for me. They told the policeman that "the man that struck him is not here, and neither are the geese here; they are both strangers to us, but this fellow has cheated the other, for he fingered the dice, and that was the way he won the geese." In the meantime the landlord asked the officer to come up and take a drink;

the officer turned to me and said: "You leave here; if you don't I will take you to the watch-house, for I know all these men don't lie." Said I, "Mr. Watchman!" Said he, "No talk out of you." This house was kept by one Mr. McDonald, a very dark man.

The next day I had such a big eye that I could not go to my service place, consequently I had to leave. I then went down to the Tombs to see if I could not have him arrested. The judge asked me if I belonged to New York. I said, "No, sir." He said, "Have you been here long?" I said, "No, sir, only five or six weeks." "Well, where are you working?" I said, "At Mrs. Lent's." "Have you ever been here before?" "Yes, sir, dozens of times." "Where do you belong when you are at home?" I told him that I belonged to Philadelphia. "So you Philadelphia niggers come here and try to whip our New York niggers, and when you cannot you try to have them arrested. Well, they have only given you a present over your eye." He then asked me if I had any money. I told him no. He then said, "Get out of my office before I give you another over the other eye." So I had to leave with my black eye. I have never raffled since, for it learned me a lesson never to go into a strange place to raffle.

A few evenings after that I was standing on the corner of Thomas street, and a man struck me with a club, and he landed me half way across the street on my knees. I never found out who he was or what it was done for, and had no suspicion of any one. About a week after, on the corner of Anthony and Broadway, I met a colored woman, and she says to me, "Come, my dear, and go home with me." I said to her, "I am greatly obliged to you, my friend; I never accompany a strange lady or ladies home, more especially when I am in a strange place." She commenced to abuse me, and I grew belligerent, and she called the watch. I ran, and as I passed the corner the watchman struck me with his mace, but I outrun him. He ran me about six blocks, but I outrun the whole party out of sight by making a warm run. I at last ran into the arms of a gentleman, and he said to me: "Tell me what the matter is, and tell me what you have done, and, if it is of no account, I will let you go." I told him the whole story, just as it was and had happened. He said, "If that is all, go; and you have done nothing more than what was right, and if I see the officers I shall turn them back." I then made a straight line for home.

A few weeks after that I went to work for George Webster, at the corner of Church and Leonard streets, who was to pay me by the week. I worked three weeks for him, but got no pay, and could get none. I figured up how much was coming to me, and went and got twenty gentlemen, and taking them to Mr. Webster's, who kept a house of entertainment, called for supper. After supper we all called for drinks. I then told him to charge it to me. He said no, he would charge it to the gentlemen. They said, "No, Mr. Williams invited us, and we came with that understanding. He then cursed at me, and said he knew that was what I was up to when I came down ahead, and for a little he would give me a good flogging. As soon as he said that I blazed away at him with tumblers, the rest following suit. In a few minutes his wife came with a kettle of hot water and he with a butcher's knife, and while the rest were in the skirmish I made for the door, which I took off from the hinges and dropped on the sidewalk.

A few evenings after that there was a gentleman rooming in the same room with me and another gentleman. This man's name was William Browne, and he seemed to have been in a fix in the night, but he is all right now. He was formerly from California.

But, reader, I have given you a sketch; let it suffice as a warning to you.

Obey the command of God—more especially the first commandment with promise: honor thy father and thy mother, that thy days may be long in the land which the Lord thy God giveth thee; keep holy the Sabbath day and live holy; deal justly with your neighbors, and strive to do good by establishing societies among your race of people; be charitable to all mankind. By doing this you will shun numerous vices you may fall into by leaving it undone.

A few days after, I was going down Leonard street, and I met a man that I knew. I said, "Hallo, Prince." He answered, "Hallo, Tom! How long have you been here?" I told him that I had been here some time. Knowing that the Fugitive Slave Law was still in force, and then seeing him, I concluded it was time for me to be leaving there. I took the cars

and went to Boston, and after remaining there some time, there came some slaveholders to arrest a slave. His name was William Craft. I armed myself on that occasion and went out to fight for him. I remained there about three weeks, and then went to New Bedford, and stayed there about three weeks, and, like a fox, I came right back to where I started from—Philadelphia. I got a situation on a freight barge, and the first morning of my cooking I drew a bucket of salt water and made coffee. The captain said, "Cook, what is the matter with the coffee? Why," said he, "you have made it out of salt water!" "No," said I. "Well, now," he said, "taste it." I did so, and after tasting, I said, "Why, captain, somebody has put salt into it, for I made it out of fresh water." "Well, where did you get the water, then?" "I drew it from the side well." "Is not that salt?" said he. "No, sir," said I. "Well, then, draw a bucket and taste it," said he. So away I went and drew it. "Take a full drink," he said. Not knowing, I took a dipper and took a hearty swallow; but I tell you I dropped it very quick, and it so amused the captain that he laughed heartily. I always knew the difference between salt and fresh water after that time.

I shall now pen a few lines of poetry. Although it is not refined, I hope you will look upon it as coming from a person that never had the privileges of an education. Being born a slave, all I can do is to venture.

> Slavery, thou cruel curse,
> > Tolerated more than two hundred years,
> Corrupted by moral laws,
> > Supported by kings and emperors.

> Thou has forced a thousand tears
> > From mothers and fathers dear—
> Whilst hearts melted from fear;
> > Hell only is thy peer.

> You flourished long enough,
> > To cultivate the coin;
> Farewell, old master,
> > Your loss is our gain.

> None but the free
> > Can enjoy themselves aright—
> None but the free
> > Can serve the Lord indeed.

> Slavery hath made a code,
> > Abridged the freeman's law;
> Reject the black, respect the white,
> > This was always slavery's code.

> Taney in his decision,
> > Confirmed this mode;
> His cruel decision
> > Supported slavery's code.

My languishing body is at rest—
   Achings and pains are o'er;
To be free is to be blessed;
   Slavery, thou art no more.

Your clinking chains are hushed,
   You cannot wear our lives away;
Toiling in the cotton and cane-bush,
   Freedom now has her sway.

And now, dear reader, I return to the place I left off at, which was concerning the coffee, made out of, or made with salt water, which I informed you I soon got tired of, and shortly after which, and whilst laying at Brooklyn, New York, there came an Irishman on board of the vessel and said to me: "Cook, come up to my house to-night; we are going to have a dance." So I went up to dance with the Irish girls, and

danced until my feet got in a perspiration, and then I took my boots off and took it barefooted, as I saw the girls doing the same. On the next day my feet were so swollen that I was not able to attend to my business for a week, and that put an end to my dancing. Thus I came to the conclusion that I would be a better man.

I further concluded that slipping and sliding would not find a place of safety in the United States. I did not want to go to Canada, because it was so cold; at least, from what I had heard, I had come to the belief that it was so cold I could not live there at all, for I had been taught to sing the old song: "Winter time, fodder-house; summer time, shady tree." And besides hearing such bad reports of starvation and knowing that I was poor, I concluded that I would go to California. Standing on the wharf one day and looking at a steamer that was going to California, the second pastry cook backed out and I agreed to take his place. The steamer's name was the North America. She sailed from New York, March 3, 1851, and after being out on the ocean three days the steward began talking pretty rough to me. I was going to whip him or give him a chance to whip me, and he went forward and told the clerk. The clerk came and told me that the steward was an officer of the vessel and that I must obey him. He pulled out his book and asked me to sign the articles. I told him no, but he said it was the rules of the ship that all seamen must sign the articles; and so long as I did not sign them I was only a passenger, working my way out, and so they could not cuff me around as they did the others whenever they felt disposed so to do.

There is no person knows what hard times the poor sailors have but those who go in vessels to traverse the briny ocean. One thing I know, the life is worse than some dogs fare in these United States. When we landed at Chagres I told the purser that I was going to California and I wanted him to pay me my money for my labor. I said to him, "Do you see anything green in my eye?" But, however, I concluded that I was even, so I picked up a pillow-case and put half a ham in it and two loaves of bread, and started over the side of the ship with it into a boat and went on shore. After I got ashore I met a Californian, and he asked me where I was going and where I came from. I told him that I came from the United States and that I was going to California, if I could get there, and that I had run away from the ship and had no money of any account. He put his hand into his pocket, gave me a ten-dollar gold piece, and told me "to keep out of the whisky shops and dance houses, and you will do well in that country."

Now this was a white man, and there were seven colored men aboard the ship, and some of them had plenty of money, but none of them did anything towards helping me along at all. When I got up Chagres river my money as gone. I had no place to sleep and no money to pay for a sleeping place. I then went down on board of the boat, turned my coat-collar up and my hat down over my eyes. The next morning one of the passengers saw me and he said: "Have those colored boys done anything for you, or have they helped you any yet?" I said, "No, sir." "Well, why don't you go and ask them?" I said, "They know I have no money or anything, and as they do not give me anything or ask how I am doing, I am not going to ask them." I knew some of them had either read or heard the following words: "Whosoever hath this world's goods and meets his brother in need, and shutteth up his bowels of compassion from him, how dwelleth the love of God in him?" He gave me a dollar and told me to go in and get my breakfast. I went in and got my breakfast and started for Panama about 4 o'clock in the afternoon, leaving the mules and two horses out all night. I went to the American Hotel and I asked the landlord if I could stop there. He said, "Yes," and the first man that got there from the boat was the man that gave me the dollar on board the boat to get my breakfast. His name was Mr. Agner. He said to me, "Clean my pants and bring me some water to wash my feet, and I will see that your bill is paid here." He then went to the landlord and said, "Give this man whatever he wants to eat and drink and I will pay it." Then the landlord turned to me and said, "I will give you seventy-five dollars a month if you will act as porter for me." I assured him that I would do so. The colored men I left behind, who come on the ship the same time, I met at the door. I said to them, "Give me your names, gentlemen; also your baggage." Said they, "Get out; where is the landlord?" "Give me your baggage and just walk into the sitting-room." But they still refused to do so. I then called the attention of the landlord, who said, "Give your baggage to this man, for he is the porter, and he is the proper representative to take care of it," which of course made me walk as though I owned all the house. You remember just the night before I had nowhere to lay my head; and being raised from that situation to the porterage of one of the finest hotels in Panama, it was a large jump. Reader, do you not think I should have been grateful for such a great beneficent benefactor? How I should strive to render due gratitude unto Him. I should say with the poet—

> How careful then ought I to live,
>   With what religious care,
> Who such a strict account must give
>   For my behavior here.

At supper time I rang the bell, and they all came down to supper, the passengers looking upon me with much astonishment. One of them, of dark hue, who had not treated me with the respect he ought to have done, said, "Hallo, Williams, how is it that you have got to be porter here?" This was done to blandish me. I then thought it was my time to treat him with the same contempt that he had treated me with on board the boat. This you know was wrong. It was not doing as my Bible taught me. I once heard of a little girl who read her Bible, and gave proof that she was governed by its precepts. The facts were these: She had been to school. On her way home she met with a little girl who always made it a point to push her out of the path. This day it pleased her teacher to give Emma, for that was her name, a great many bunches of grapes, and on her way home, as usual, she came in contact with the other little girl, and she gave this same little girl some of them. Going home she told her mother concerning the grapes, and she said to her, "I think your teacher was very kind to give you so many." She told her mother that that was not all she could tell her; for she had given some to a little girl who always pushed her out of the path.

I said to the man, "That is my business, sir, and not for you to know." They staid in the house about six days. Then they got a chance to take the old steamship Republic. Henry Smith went on board as steward. One man of dark complexion among the crowd said, "I will speak to Mr. Smith to get you a situation on board." I said, "Thank you, sir." Mr. Smith came to me, falling back on his dignity, after he had been accosted about me. Speaking to me in a very high tone of voice and with authority, he said, "Mr. So-and-So," calling the gentleman by name, "has been talking to me about your wanting to go to California." Says he, "The rest of the boys have all been employed, but if you want to go I will give a billet, though the boys have been given wages, if you will work your passage." I paused a few moments. Seeing there were hundreds of people here wanting to go and could not get a passage to California from this place, I soon reflected and accepted the billet, having an idea that I could do so much better if I could reach California. After I had started and went on board of the ship with him and had been set to work, I remembered that I had a lot of Mr. Agner's clothes at the washerwoman's, and he knew not where they were, and he had been so good to me, so I started to go ashore to take the clothes to him. I spoke to the second steward, and he gave me permission to go and do so. While on shore I met the head steward, Mr. Smith. He cursed me because I came ashore, and said I had no right there. It made no matter who gave me permission unless it came from him. He said, "You shall not go in the ship, so you may stay here." A few of the passengers gathered

around and heard him talking to me and were going to club him. I went back and told Mr. Agner what happened, and he said, "Never mind; it is all right. I will pay your passage out to California in the Jenny Lind." He paused for a few moments, after which he wrote a note to Captain Hudson. The captain looked at the note, and then said, "I thought you went aboard in the steward's boat last night?" "I did, sir," said I, "but the steward said I should not go in the ship because I came ashore to get Mr. Agner's clothes that I had taken to the washerwoman's for him." "Then," says he, "you may go and wait on the doctor. Doctor," says he, "you take this man to wait on you," and away I went on board of the ship again. The steward came to me and said, "What are you doing on board here, sir? Get ashore." I said, "I will not do it, sir." "Then," said he, "have you paid your fare?" Said I, "That is none of your business." He then said, "All right; I will find out," and off he goes to the clerk. The clerk said to him, "This man is all right, steward, never mind him." The next morning early the steward came to me and said, "Williams, come here, I want you to take charge of the first and second officers' state-rooms, and I want you to keep them clean." I saw the low cunning and dirty trick in giving me rooms that I could not make a cent off of them. I said to him, "I will not do it," and he said he would have me put in the coal-hole right away, and away he started off. The captain said, "What is the matter with you, Williams, that you cannot obey the steward?" I said to him, "The steward did not want me to come on board here, and now he wants me to do a whole lot of work, and the doctor told me not to obey any one except the first officer, the clerk or himself." Then said the captain to me, "The steward is an officer of the ship, and if you have any time to do anything he asks you to do, do it." He then turned to the steward and said, "Steward, you have no control over this man; he belongs to the doctor." I, therefore, never had any time to do anything for him, and I was a complete pet among the passengers. They gave me money and they also gave me six boxes of wine. One man of dark hue, who was steerage steward, whose name was William Nutter, from Boston, came to me to buy this wine. He had no money, but the steward went his security. This was done to cheat me, but I was not aware of it. After we were out about six days the saloon waiter was taken sick and I had to doctor him. I noticed one day that the head steward, the second steward and the storekeeper were drinking a bottle of champagne wine. The head steward called me and gave me a glass. This he done to deceive me, and he said, at the same time, "I am very sorry that I did not hire you and put you on wages," and he said to me, "Won't you come down and wait on the captain's dinner, and I will fix it so that you can get a little money from the ship." I done so the next day. He said to me, "Williams, if you will take these state-rooms and take care of them you will be able to make something off of them, for I see you are the best man in the ship," and I, being inexperienced at the time and anxious to make all that I could, bit at the bait, but never ate it. I never made a cent for my time or labor, so you can see what a man that has made his escape from the blood-hounds hath to undergo to reach the shores of California, where he could be free and safe from all danger of being apprehended. Whilst in that country I saw some that I had to run away from, yet I would have you to understand that I had no running away to do in California. The boat was caught in a gale and we were four weeks getting from Panama to San Francisco.

On the 15th day of May, 1851, I took a little boat, called the Jenny Lind, and came to Sacramento, and I then started to the mines. The first place I came to was called Negro Hills. I worked there some time and made nothing but my board. At that time there were no stages in

the country at all, and we miners had to go on horseback and on foot. I made up my mind to leave this part of the diggings. I did so and started for Kelsey's Diggings. I packed my rocker that we washed the gold with, my prospect-pan, and my pick and shovel, and led the way. I started over the hills and valleys, prospecting for gold, and my bed, when night came on, was under some cedar tree, and I had to pack my grub under my head to keep the wolves and coyotes from stealing it. We had no law in the country at that time and we miners constituted a law for ourselves. I was one of the miners that was present on an occasion to try another miner for the crime of stealing $50 from another. We put a rope around his neck and intended to frighten him, and he said if we let him down he would tell. So we let him down and he went and got the money. Had he not got the money, what the result would have been I am unable to tell the reader. One thing I am about to affirm, I would never have consented to have taken the man's life. I was the only colored man in the crowd, and it was left for me to pass my opinion, and I said, "If he gives up the money let him go," for I felt greatly opposed to taking the man's life; yet in a body of men there are always different opinions, and I do not think the poor fellow would have had much lenity shown to him, it being thought a very dastardly trick for one miner to steal from another.

Any man that made up his mind to go to the mines at that time, he must be a man that feared no noise, or else he had better stay at home, for the miners feared no noise at that time, it being a newly-settled country, with wild beasts and also wild people. I belonging to the party that believed in liberty, it made me a little wild also. Persons living in places where they have to be a law to themselves are, of course, nearly or quite as apt to resort to very stringent laws as the more sure remedy to lessen crime. Whether it be the fact or not, it requires thought, as time expounds all miracles, and it takes time to tell about that. However, the state of things is much better now in California than was the case on my arrival there. Many adventures have been made by persons from the States, colored and white. There are now instances on record where both classes have gathered considerable of this world's goods. Some are now enjoying the benefits of their labor, whilst others, who worked hard in the mines and have gathered a large portion of this world's goods and have had no advantage, neither will they ever reap any advantage hereafter from their privations, although they have borne the burden in the heat of the day—collected the spoils; but, ah, they have sown sparingly—they have sowed the good seed sparingly, I mean; but ill-gotten means never stay long with the receiver. Some have plundered and robbed, perhaps I may say truthfully, murdered; anyway, just so that I get—no matter about the remaining—just so I get my booty,

I have never for a moment thought of wronging any one out of their dues. That is what made me so bitter against slaveholders. By reading this book, ere this you are convinced that I have been bitter against such men. But for the Emancipation Proclamation I should be the same this day, although, like many others, I have been accused through life falsely.

On the 15th day of May, A.D. 1851, you have learned I arrived in the city of Sacramento. You have also learned that I worked in the gold mines called Nigger Hills. I worked there about six months, and seeing nothing could be made there I left and went to Kelsey's Diggings. I worked there about three months, with no better success. I then returned to the city of Sacramento. I there commenced carrying the hod, which I did for three months, at six dollars per day, after which I bought out the good-will and fixtures of a large restaurant, and kept it for the entertainment of the whites. Be it known that about that time there was a number of slaves brought to California by their masters, one of which was a woman, brought there by her master, who would not allow one man or men to go to his house. But I went there, taking a white man with me at the time, and took her away. In a few days her master comes to my establishment, bringing with him an officer, who presented a pistol at me, saying at the same time, "Williams, you must go and get that woman you stole from Mr. Wholeman or I will blow your brains out." "Very good, sir," says I, "come on," I leading the way. Taking him direct into lawyer Zabriskie's office I alleged my complaint against him for pointing a six-shooter at me, and he was held for trial, which was given in my favor. Of course I retained her, and in one week after this woman left and went back to her master, telling him that I threatened to shoot him. His party getting after me caused me to leave there, and on the boat plying between Sacramento and San Francisco I was attacked by a party of Missourians and beaten very badly, and had to be rescued by the captain, after having run into the ladies' saloon.

From thence I took the boat and went to Mexico. From Mexico I went to Guaymas, and there I was robbed by a woman, I seeing her when she committed the robbery whilst I was laying in bed. I arose in the morning, and, after having dressed myself, went to her room and knocked at the door. I told her I wanted her to give me my money. She soon went and brought her brother, who informed me, if I said that his sister robbed me he would cut my head off. I told him that I did not say so. He then told me that I must treat him. I had only $2.50. However, I treated him, and I was left without money, and I had to be out some three or four weeks without any means at all to depend upon. I at last got a chance to work my passage to Mazatlan, and on arriving there, without anything or any money, all I had to live on was a sixpence per day, and the way I procured that was, I in general begged it from the sailors. At this time I sold my coat, the only one I had got. Having but one shirt, I used to go to the shore and wash it, and lay there until it was dry. The bed I laid on was the ground. Often were the times when the police wanted to arrest me, but I would not consent, because I said to him, "The earth only is my bed, the canopy my covering, and often a rock my pillow." Thus you see how I got along so far. Be it known that I at this time had a chum, a white man. He and I agreed to ship and go to Talcahuana. We did so by shipping in a bark named the Calilena. The captain's name was Wilson, known then by the name of Bully Wilson, from the fact that he was said to flog all the sailors he hired. I and my partner concluded that, as it only took two months to make the trip, we could make the voyage with him, as we said we could live with Old Sammy three months. On the voyage he flogged all hands except us. We concluded, as a matter of course, that our turn was next. Accordingly, we fixed our mind in this way, that if he flogged one he must be man enough to flog both. At length he commenced with me, and my chum seconded the motion, and we had a free thing of it. In the melée I received a mark that I shall carry to my grave. However, we made port. The crew was arraigned for mutiny, or, however, he discharged all the crew except me and my chum. Him he put in prison for mutiny and me he retained on board. I told him, after he had hired a Spanish crew, he had broke the articles of agreement, and he must discharge me. But he would not, saying that he could not do without me. Consequently, I that night ran away from the ship. As a matter of course he had to get a Spanish cook and leave. But before he left he saw the American Consul, and advised him, when I came in town, to have me arrested and tried, and, if found guilty, to make me serve out my time in the prison or chain-gang. Luckily, I could take the Spanish language, and I gained the favor of the chief officer, and by his means my chum and I were released from prison, and I reshipped in a ship named Kate Hayes for California, and after I had shipped on board of the above-named vessel, learning that I had shipped with another bad man, I did, as I always think of doing, making the best of a bad bargain. I found there was no error in the report, for no sooner than the first or second morning did I receive a partial chastisement from him. I bore with him until I was some five or six days out at sea, when, one morning, I made up my mind that I was now safe to carry out my designs. Accordingly, he had been told by the mate to let me alone, but he would not. I turned on him one morning, and after fighting some time, I, after being called to by the mate, related my grievance to him, but still kept on fighting. The mate called the captain, who, after seeing the situation, said that we should fight it out. Finding him rather good for a knock down, I gathered him for a rough and tumble—as used to be the common way of fighting. After throwing him, I struck him whilst down. The captain then struck me with a main brace, and I ran and refused to fight; he made me come back, for he had called all of the passengers to witness the fight, and declared that we should fight it out on that line, as General Grant said. I went back and commenced the old field-fight. Reader, are you aware of the old field-fight what it is? I mean butting; and I held him and butted him until he sang an old song—which was murder. I tell you, after that I had peace. Arriving at San Francisco in the fall '53, I there found civil law established. Then I concluded that I could remain, and not be molested by Copperheads or Southern sympathizers, as I had been before. I then concluded to make my abode there for awhile, and therefore I did. I returned back in the fall of '53, as you have learned. In '54 I was private watchman for James King of Wm., who was killed by Casey, who was afterwards hung by the Vigilance Committee for the crime in '55. I then returned to Sacramento, and came to the conclusion that I would get work on the Levee, but as no colored persons had ever worked there, it was determined that I should not, and after repeated interruptions, which resulted in suits at law, and me paying fines, having my property destroyed, etc., and at length fights, I proved my determination to them, and they gave me countenance. Since which time the way, through my determination, hath been opened, and colored men can now work on the Levee, as much so as white men, and be respected in their doings.

It must be acknowledged by all that the credit is due to me for opening the way successfully, by hardships endured by me, like a good soldier, having witnessed the bad usage of colored men on the Levee. This will be understood to have been done previous to the state of things as they now exist; I am aware such is not the case now. I speak of the time when such law as existed in the State of Delaware, prior to the passage of the Civil Rights Bill, when the oath of a black man was objected to, and the court was bound to sustain the objection. Agreeable to the pending law, the colored people were not allowed their oath against a white man. Now we have rights of oath in the civil courts; thank God for that.

I then went to work in the Southern mines for a man, at $100 per month, and, after working for him some six months, he either raised a false report or caused one to be raised, in order to get a certain class of men to pursue me, to make me leave the place, to elude paying me my money, and he accomplished his design. Meeting him sometime after, and asking him for my money, he told me that were he me, he would not want any money—that I should be glad that I got off with my life, much less receiving any money.

In '56 I returned to Sacramento again, and kept a junk-store on Second street. During the same year I sold out my store, and went to driving an express wagon, and remained sometime at that business. In '57—I suppose the reader perhaps has heard concerning the Archy case, which was the arrest, and an attempt to remand the said Archy, he being, at that time, a slave. I was the first man in the fray, which occurred on the night of the attempted arrest, which was consummated, and they gained the suit; yet we succeeded in rescuing the man, and sent him to Vancouver Island, and he, Archy, is now a resident of Sacramento. Boarding in the house together, I, his fellow, who aided in the rescue, we have talked over the matter often. I feel proud of the few I have aided to escape from slavery. I know the ills of it, though I was young when I cast off the yoke of bondage from my shoulder, feeling myself a little larger. Thinking, with a number of my colored friends, that I would like to breathe purer air, I, with a number, emigrated to Vancouver Island, where we thought the air was more pure; but on arriving there, finding the air somewhat tainted, I returned back to Sacramento, and went back to my old business, driving an express wagon. I remained in this business until '59, when the Washoe excitement broke out. I caught the fever also and sold out, and all the money that I gained by sale I spent in provisions and started. I met persons returning who had started, and they informed me that I could never arrive at the place. I had determined to go to Virginia City, Washoe. I arrived at Strawberry Valley, in which there was a great many persons, who had arrived there before me, and it looked doubtful to any one. Yet having all I owned at stake, besides having borrowed some fifty dollars, and being broke, I resolved to trust in God and go and see the end or die in the attempt. There was a good bed of snow on the ground. Having two horses with me, I provided as best I could and lay down on the ground. In the morning I was covered with snow, and my horses also. After repeated entreaties not to attempt it, I, with several others, started through the snow, and at times our horses were down and up; yet we crossed the summit and made the quickest trip on record. But it was through much fatigue. We encamped in the Valley of Genoa, proving by demonstration that a man cannot tell what he can endure until he puts his might into his will. After we recruited, we started for Virginia City, and after arriving there the people ran to meet us to purchase the produce which we had. Flour at that time was worth one dollar per pound. We disposed of what we had, I realizing three hundred dollars for what flour I had. To the best of my judgment I disposed of the produce, and after being fully satisfied with my adventure, I tried to make as good an observation of the surroundings as I could, viewing with the utmost precaution all that came under my notice, which I will defer saying anything about at present.

Reader, I have lived long; have traveled in numerous parts of the world; have observed many things. I have learned things that would perhaps be of great service to many that this little treatise may fall into the hands of. I have learned to strive to live as peaceably as lieth in my power with all persons, to insure safety of person, for better is it to have the good favor of a dog than the ill-will of him, for I have learned, by ill-using him, that he will remember the abuse. I have learned by experience that kindness is never forgotten by the creature. He has been known to think of or remember his master so much or so long, that, when his master hath been borne to the grave, he hath followed the procession. He has carried his young master's toys and playthings, scratched a hole in the earth where the body was deposited, and put them in; after being confined to prevent this recurring, he has moaned, in his way, until he has been released, and has then refused to eat, and finally has stretched himself on the grave, and there remained until he expired. Could it be thought for a moment that ill-usage ever caused him to do this? I answer, no! I have learned this by experience.

I have told you, ere this, concerning a gentleman who gave me a ten-dollar gold piece when in a strange country, out of money and friends, for all was strange to me. Think you I can ever forget the act of kindness that gentleman done me? No. I could not think of ever forgetting it. I have met several gentlemen that I always shall remember, and when, at my secret devotions, they appear foremost in my mind, oh, how bright they do appear! It seems that I carry them to the haven of eternal repose. I also have learned that I must, if I expect friends, show myself friendly, for it is a fact uncontradicted successfully. I have learned, experimentally, if I act selfishly with persons I need expect nothing short of it. Believe me, the man of generosity receives the same. Says the teacher of Christianity, be kind and affectionate one to another, not begrudging; that is not the way to receive generosity, by no means. Let this be remembered, dear reader, you may be in the situation that I have been in before now, surrounded by strangers, not one cent in your pocket, and not a place to lay your head; you will then wish to come across a friend—one who will take you upon his own breast and take you to an inn, and say to the landlord: "Take care of this man or woman, and when I return I will pay you." Oh, what joy would spring up in your heart! I have witnessed the like myself by my own experience, when in a strange land. Further, in my travels I have found out, to my satisfaction, that to command the respect of others or from others, one lesson I must first learn, that is to respect myself, which implies respect begetteth respect. For if the individuals first respect themselves others will respect them in turn. I have found the same in all my journeys through life. In all places that I have been in the rule holds to be the same. Reader, respect yourself, and you will be respected. You will live "that the world may be made better by you, and you will die regretted by all who endeavor to respect themselves." After I had made my escape from one of the American slaveholders, whose name I have given you, I walked by the same rule I have endeavored to lay down here for you to govern yourself by, and I never give advice to anyone unless I first proved the same to be good for the receiver. Thus my rule is, first to be sure that I am right, then go ahead. It is the only sure road to the summit for all who wish to rise in life.

I previously promised to tell you more about Washoe. After I had sold my flour, I thought that I would purchase some land there, but after inquiry, I found the customs did not suit me, as I learned that shooting was the order of the day. If there would be a bargain effected with a party, and there arose any misunderstanding, redress appeared to be only had by shooting. I found that would not suit me at all. I then relinquished the thought of buying land in that place. I then went to Carson City, but ere I went there I returned to Sacramento, and made another trip, and was caught in a storm and lost all of my produce, but after arriving at Carson City I sold one horse and bought six lots, and then went to work by hand. This was done in '60. During the same year there was a flood in Sacramento, and I, at that time, owned a house there. That was washed away. After working by hand some two months and receiving nothing, the customs being such, I returned to California, and remained there until '63, at my old business. I then went back to Carson City, and sold the property owned by me. I then went to Virginia City, and bought six lots, and went back in '65 and sold two lots, realizing $2,500 for them. I then returned to California, and got a billet on board of the cars, and held it for two months. I was then taken sick, and so remained for eighteen months, and so I lost my billet. In the year 1867 I was appointed agent and collector by the trustees of A. M. E. Church in the city of Sacramento, and acknowledged by the then elder—now Bishop Ward—as agent, collector and superintendent of the above church, and I went forward and I built the church, yet, like all other great undertakings by man, the credit that was due me I did not get. The reader is aware of the fact that, when in public life, we cannot get the praise due us in our undertakings. I finished the church, receiving for my labor two dollars per day, traveling expenses, board and all paid me. I held the above office until '69, when I settled up and resigned my situation. There was now a situation awaiting for me to accept—the agency of the building or collecting for and superintending the building of another A. M. E. church in San Francisco, on my return there, which I call my home. I thought, in this short treatise, I would give my experience, and the treatment which I have met with. I have never had the privilege of attending school, being born a slave, and not having the chance of education. Having been informed, in part, what education would do for me, how I have wished to be young again, and have the privilege of going to school! I have been told a great deal about its effects. It is said by one, I am informed, that the term education, when employed in its primitive sense and literal signification, means the drawing out or development of the human faculties. When we look on a child we perceive at once that, besides corporeal organs and powers, he has a spiritual nature, in which these organs act themselves, but not an unmeaning activity. We see that this little being has intelligence, sensibility and will. Such powers exist in early infancy but as germs, which are destined, however, to burst forth, and which, like the vegetating powers of the seed that we have planted, are ready to be directed and controlled by us almost at our will. As we can train to a healthy and graceful maturity the young plant, which, if neglected, would have proved unsightly and sterile, so we can train up in the way he should go that child, who, if left to himself, would have almost been vicious and ignorant. It is the peculiar liability and impressibility of this early period of life that gives it such claims on the educator, whether his intellectual or his moral powers can hold intercourse with or act upon the world without, except through the material organs. And, in our present state these organs are also necessary to the soul, even in its more spiritual operations, and they weigh it down to imbecility whenever they become greatly diseased or enfeebled. When habit has once fastened itself on the intellect or the heart, and the heart's appeals and influences are comparatively powerless, in whatever degree, then it may be our interest and duty to promote the welfare of our fellow-creatures, and especially of our own children, in some degree. Thus it becomes important that we lose no portion of that precious seed-time of their lives. Hardly any season is too early for the culture of this soil, and if it would be reckoned the height of guilt to refuse food or raiment of the body to a helpless little one, what must be that cruel neglect which leaves its nobler nature to pine, and finally to perish for lack of knowledge? Educated, in one sense, this child will be for weal or woe.

> For nature's crescent does not grow alone
> In thews and bulks, but as this temple wears,
> The inward service of the mind and soul
> Grows wide withal.

It is for the parent or guardian to decide what character this development shall take. The power of education we are not disposed to overrate. It has sometimes been described, even by wise men, as an all-prevailing element or agent, which can turn the minds of children as easily this way or that as water itself, and before which all original differences may be made to disappear. It seems to us that a slight acquaintance with children is sufficient to refute this story or theory. Even when reared in the same family, and subject to the same course of physical and moral training, they exhibit, amid a general resemblance in manners and principles, the greatest diversity of endowments and dispositions. It is evidently not to be desired that all men and women should be cast in the same intellectual more than in the same corporeal mould. And hence, though compounded of the same primitive elements, these elements have been so variously mingled and combined, that each individual has his own peculiar and indestructible nature, as well as his own sphere of action, and thus every place and calling can be filled. As this variety then exists, and never can be entirely effaced, it ought to be respected in education; but does it follow that the work of education is, therefore, slight or unimportant, while we are bound to take the individual as he is? And having his peculiar type of character and measure of capacity to keep these ever in view, is there not still a vast work to be accomplished? It is the business of education to watch the dormant powers, and foster their healthy and well-proportioned growth; restraining and repressing where their natural activity is too great and stimulating where they are too feeble. To respect each one's individuality is not only consistent with this great work, but is indispensable to its highest success. Doing so, we can effect vast changes and improvements in character; the sluggish we may not be able to inspire with great vivacity, nor subdue the ardent or enthusiastic to the tone and calm of a calculating spirit, but we can arrest the dangerous tendencies in each. We can correct mental obliquities and distortions, and cultivate a healthy and self-improving power. We can study the purposes of the Creator in framing such a mind, and strive wisely as well as unceasingly to fulfill those purposes. In a word, we can labor to rear this child, yet without fixed character or compacted energies, to the stature of a perfect man or woman. As one star is different from another star in magnitude and splendor, though each in its appointed place is equally perfect, so, in the intellectual firmament, one mind may outshine another, and yet both alike be perfect in their sphere, and in fulfilling the missions assigned by God. Milton has called that a complete and generous education which fits a man to perform justly, skillfully and magnanimously all the offices, both private and public, of peace and of war. It is evident that such an education can be enjoyed only by a few, and that, though enjoyed by all, it would bestow on but a limited number the lofty capacities indicated by the great poet. A vast proportion of the walks of human life are humble and sheltered. Let us be grateful, however, that, while in such walks we escape the fiery trials which await those who tread the high places of earth, they still afford scope and opportunity for the exercise of the most manly and generous qualities. He may be great both mentally and intellectually who has filled no distinguished office, either of peace or war. Let it rather be our object, then, in rearing the young, to form a perfect character, to build up a spirit of which all must say, as was said of Brutus by Anthony:

> His life was gentle, and the elements
> So mixed in him, that nature might stand up
> And say to all the world, this was a man.

I have here narrated a few simple facts of what some men of literary attainments call education, and by me, perusing as well as I could, it gives me a faint glimpse of what I might have been if I had been sent to school when young; and by perusing this little treatise you may consider, as I have, that no one can tell what they can do, if they only have a mind. As we often say, where there is a will to do there always is a way to perform. I am of opinion that such language is nothing but fact, incontrovertible, successfully. Let some who are in the habit of saying, "I cannot," use the word, "I will try;" make the effort, and I assure you that you will succeed in all laudable endeavors. I once learned of a certain lady who hired a cook who was smart, and she would always get her work done, and had time to sit, walk out or sew in the afternoon. At length she left her place, and the lady had to employ another, who was not so smart, and, as is usually the custom, the lady said to the servant, "How is it you are always at work and never have any time? Why, Biddy always was done and out walking, or sitting sewing, or resting herself." The girl was anxious to know how she could do it. "Oh," said the lady, "perseverance." The next day the family had apple-dumplings for dinner; there were eight left; the girl sat down to her dinner, and ate them all. Towards evening, the lady, feeling as though she would like to have an apple-dumpling, said to Biddy, "Please give me one of the apple-dumplings, that was left from dinner." "Oh," she said, "I ate them." "Why," said the lady, "did you eat all of them?" "Yes, madam," said Biddy. "How did you manage to eat them all?" "Oh," said Biddy, "perseverance, madam, perseverance. Is not that the way you told me? The girl done the work and rested or sewed or walked out in the afternoon. I ate the dumplings—only eight—and I have rested since then, and I think, if I continue persevering, I will just do like the other girl did, after awhile." It is generally the case in whatever we undertake; if we strive to we can do it by perseverance. Allow me to say to you, reader, let your motto be, "Press on." If misfortune assail, press on; the rougher the way the shorter—press on. If the sky is cloudy, it will be clear sometime—press on. If you cannot get far, go on as far as you can, thinking "man's extremity is God's opportunity." He will make use of it, and bring you out in a way that you are not aware of, and, as the poet says, when viewing his forlorn situation,

> "Ten thousand foes around my feet,
>   Not one shall hold me fast;
> Through every trouble I shall meet
>   I shall be safe at last."

Take the watchword and go on. I am telling you to do what you have already learned that I have done. I have been without money, and I have been cast out in a strange land amongst strangers, without means. I kept on; I strove to keep my head above the current. I did so. I have done all in my power to get an honest living. I have been as charitable as it has been in my power. Doing all the good I could, and the Lord has blessed my efforts, and I am still living, and although I have been near the water's edge, the water has never overflowed me; and I am still floating on the current with my head above water. I hope, my reader, that you will take fresh courage and press on, as the day will soon break. We live in an age of progress—in the same age we were created. In the way the world was created, progress was the order of the creation. I am convinced of the fact and am led to believe that many of my readers are convinced of the same thing. How thankful I am that I am no worse off than I am; although I have been very ungrateful to my Heavenly Father, yet he has favored me, and had I been dealt with according to my just deserts I should be this day crying for water to cool my tongue. I think all with me will say the same, if they look back upon their past lives. We may not be what we should be, but having such a kind Benefactor we always receive more than we are worthy to receive. I always have to acknowledge this to be the manner that I am treated by my Heavenly Creator. My dear readers, I feel that all of my new imperfections will be overlooked by your kindness, more especially when you think of the chances that I have been deprived of by my once-called master. The time I should have been attending school I had to be dodging and running to keep out of the way from him, and sleep like a cat, as I before told you, with one eye open and the other eye not shut, and be ever ready to run or walk further than he or his party, or be captured. I have told you of many narrow chances of escape, and if you had seen me some of the times you would certainly have said that he is gone this time, for they certainly thought they had me, and I thought so too. But out of all the snares the Lord brought me, and was bringing me at all times in a way that I knew not of; and I am glad such has been my case. Had I been left to my own free will, I would perhaps have been done for long ago, and been in abject, or worse than abject slavery again. Let us, the colored people, begin—we that never have begun—now commence to live, that the world may be made better by us. In the course of seven or more years we have had a great deal done. Consider our case, dear reader, and just think of our situation, being that of American slavery for over two hundred years. Had the Anglo-Saxon race been held in bondage the same length of time, underwent the same hardships, the same privations, been deprived of their privileges, knocked and cuffed about, husbands and wives separated, and children and parents, which will take almost the same length of time to bring them together again—nay, may I say, they never can be brought together again. There are children of one parent who never more will know each other, perhaps working in the same field together, yet they were separated when they were so young they could never know or remember each other. Think of it, the Anglo-Saxon race, had they been under the same yoke, would they this day be any better than we are? Would they be any more intelligent than we? Would they be any more civilized, any more Christianized than we are? I am aware that we are in the woods. I am aware that we are in the wilderness! But, ah! whose fault is it? Is it because we could not learn? Is it because we had the opportunity and would not learn? Is it because we idled our time away and would not work? Nay, we were beat. Some of our people have been whipped to death, some have been tortured in other ways. We have done nothing worthy of such treatment. We have always acted better than we have been treated. We have always acted better than the Anglo-Saxon would have acted; yet we need not tell them. They know; here and there one of them will confess. All of our bad deeds we have learned from him. Tell me of one thing done by a colored man that the same has not been done by a white man! I know of not even one, from the least to the greatest crime on record. If I could only think of a crime that my race had been guilty of doing that the Anglo-Saxon had not done, I would mention it. But memory fails to remember. I conclude thus, that nothing that ever the colored man ever did, good or bad, but the white man had done before him. I mean, since the colored man was first brought to this country by him, the white man, and used in the manner he has been by him. And then he, the white man, having the daring impudence to say that "We have done your race good." It is now evident that the two races cannot live together. This is a white man's government. A "colored man has no rights that a white man is bound to respect." Father, forgive them, for they are not aware of what they are saying. I mean, they are not aware of the extent or import of what other people infer from what they say. On or about the year A.D. 1838, I gave Mr. William Hollingsworth leg-bail for security, and in the year 1869 I went to redeem my bail. I found the slave-mart done away with; I also found the jail, called by and after the fiend in human shape at that time, Woodforks. What shape he is in now I cannot tell, and am not anxious to know. But I find that there is a fine dwelling erected on the site of the old prison, and the old whipping-post rotted down—grass all growing in the place. What an alteration has taken place since I used to visit the old place! I am very fond of going there looking at the scenery of the place. It does me good. None but a wonder-working God could have accomplished all this in the manner that this was done. Well may it be said that this is an age of wonders. Well may it be said that the world is changing, and we are changing with it, and I hope that it will keep on undergoing a change until it is made what the Creator will have it. It will then be right, for whatever He doeth is right, and whenever He doeth it is the time it should be done. Thus He has commenced. All that is essential for us to do, is to stand still and see the salvation of God. I do not mean by saying stand still, to do nothing. That is not my meaning. I mean to do and try to act right; live godly in Christ Jesus. Suffer persecution; fight the good fight—I mean for you to lay hold on eternal life—that is what I mean by standing still. And when you are standing still and running at the same time, you are running so as to obtain—you are walking and not fainting. I counsel strong on this point. I mean for you to own your name in the gathering morning, when burning worlds shall dash together; when the scattered elements shall be collected; that is the time I mean. I have thought that at this time it would be very proper to quote the Mission of the Flowers, penned by Mrs. F. A. Harper:

"In a lovely garden, filled with fair and blooming flowers, stood a beautiful rose-bush or tree; it was the centre of attraction, and won the admiration of every eye. Its beauteous flowers were sought to adorn the bridal wreath and deck the funeral bier. It was a thing of joy, and its earth-mission was a blessing. Kind hands plucked its flowers to gladden the chamber of sickness, and to adorn the prisoner's cell. Young girls

wore it amidst their clustering curls, and grave brows relaxed when they
gazed upon their wondrous beauty. Now, the rose was very kind and
generous-hearted, and seeing how much joy she dispensed, wished that
every flower could only be a rose, and like herself, have the privilege of
giving joy to the children of men. While she thus mused, a bright and
lovely spirit approached her, and said, 'I know thy wishes and will grant
thy desires. Thou shalt have power to change every flower in the garden
to thine own likeness. When the soft winds come wooing thy fairest buds
and flowers, thou shalt breathe gently on thy sister plants, and beneath
thy influence they shall change to beautiful roses.' The rose-tree bowed

her head in silent gratitude to the gentle being who had granted her
this wondrous power. All night the stars bent over her, from their holy
homes, but she scarcely heeded their vigils. The gentle dews nestled in
her arms, and kissed the cheeks of her daughters, but she hardly noticed
them. She was waiting for the soft airs to awaken and seek her charming
abode. At length the gentle airs greeted her, and she hailed them with
a joyous welcome, and then commenced the work of change. The first
object which met her vision was a tulip, superbly arrayed in scarlet and
gold. When she was aware of the intention of her neighbor, her cheeks

flamed, her eyes flashed indignantly, and she haughtily refused to change her proud robes for the garb the rose-tree had prepared for her, but she could not resist the spell that was upon her, and she passively permitted the garments of the rose to enfold her yielding limbs. The verbenas saw the change that had fallen upon the tulip, and, dreading that a similar fate awaited them, crept closely to the ground, and while tears gathered in their eyes, they felt a change pass through their sensitive frames, and instead of gentle verbenas they were blushing roses. She breathed upon the sleeping poppies, and a deeper slumber fell upon their senses, and when they awoke they, too, had changed to bright and beautiful roses. The heliotrope read her fate in the lot of her sisters, and bowing her fair head in silent sorrow, gracefully submitted to her unwelcome destiny. The violets, whose mission was to herald the approach of spring, were averse to losing their identity. Surely, said they, we have a mission as well as the rose; but with heavy hearts they saw themselves changed, like their sister plants. The snowdrop drew around her her robes of virgin white; she would not willingly exchange them for the most brilliant attire that ever decked a flower's form. To her they were the emblems of purity and innocence, but the rose-tree breathed upon her, and, with a bitter sob, she reluctantly consented to the change. The dahlias lifted their heads proudly and defiantly; they dreaded the change, but scorned submission. They loved the fading year, and wished to spread around his dying couch their brightest, fairest flowers; but vainly they struggled; the doom was upon them, and they could not escape. A modest lily that grew near the rose shrank instinctively from her, but it was in vain, and with tearful eyes and trembling limbs she yielded, while a quiver of agony convulsed her frame. The marigold sighed submissively, and made no remonstrance. The garden pinks grew careless, and submitted without a murmur, while other flowers, less fragrant or less fair, paled with sorrow, or reddened with anger. But the spell of the rose-tree was upon them, and every flower was changed by her power, and that once beautiful garden was overrun with roses. The garden had changed, but that variety which had lent it so much beauty was gone and men grew tired of roses, for they were everywhere. The smallest violet, peeping faintly from its bed, would have been welcome. The humblest primrose would have been hailed with delight. Even a dandelion would have been a harbinger of joy. When the rose-tree saw that the children of men were dissatisfied with the change she had made, her heart grew sad within her, and she wished the power had never been given her to change her sister plants to roses. And tears came into her eyes as she mused, when suddenly a rough wind shook her drooping form and she opened her eyes, and found that she had only been dreaming. But an important lesson had been taught. She had learned to respect the individuality of her sister flowers, and she began to see that they as well as herself had their own missions. Some to gladden the eye with their loveliness and thrill the soul with delight; some to transmit fragrance to the air; others to breathe a refining influence upon the world; some had power to lull the aching brow and soothe the weary heart and brain in forgetfulness; and of those whose mission she did not understand, she wisely concluded there must be some object in their creation, and resolved to be true to her own earth-mission, and lay her fairest buds and flowers upon the altars of love and truth."

In conclusion, I have crossed the ocean some four times. Going to California and returning by the Chagres river, the scenery is very beautiful, and pays the traveler for his trouble and expense. In coming back, in 1869, I came across the plains on the railroad, which is a splendid road—a grand scene to witness: having an opportunity of seeing wild beasts and the wonderful characteristics of human nature.

Sacramento, —— ——.

In 1869 I was in Washington, and present when Senator Revels was sworn in as a United States Senator. In 1870 I was in Philadelphia, and walked in the first procession of the celebration of the passage of the Fifteenth Amendment. On March 31st, three days after, about seven o'clock in the evening, I was walking up Second street, near Market. As I was crossing the street, I was attacked by three white rowdies. One said: "Get out of the way, you damned black Fifteenth Amendment," and at the same time striking at me and missing me, when I ran into a store, and the storekeeper asked me what was the matter, and I said, "A lot of rowdies are after me;" and he told me to go out. I said, "No; there is rowdies after me;" and he said, "Go out, go out. I don't care a damn. I

am not going to have them break up the things in my store." And with
that he shoved me out, and as he shoved me out, one of them struck me
with a slung-shot near the corner of the eye. I, having a hickory cane in
my hand, at the same time struck one of the parties and felled him to
the ground. Then I broke and ran and cried, "Watch! watch!" I met a
policeman, and told him there was a lot of rowdies after me, and asked
him to go with me and arrest them. We went back, and found the man
that I had struck, up a little alley, bleeding. The officer asked him what
was the matter, and he said that he did not know. The officer asked him
who struck him, and he answered, "I don't know." I spoke up that I
struck him—"that is who struck you." Says the officer, "What did this
colored man strike you for?" He said, "I don't know, sir." One of his
companions was standing by, and he stepped up to me and said, "Who
struck you?" I said, "You did, with that slung-shot you have in your
pocket." He said, "No, sir; I did not do any such a thing." I said, "Yes,
you did." A very respectable merchant stepped up and said, "Officer,
I was in the act of crossing the street and saw the whole affray. This
colored man was coming along peaceably and these fellows attacked
him. I halted on the corner and saw this fellow strike him, and then
he ran around the corner and comes back and asks who struck him."
I said to the officer, "Arrest them and take them to the watch-house."
The officer stepped up to me softly and said, "Step here; I want to speak
to you a minute. You gave them just as good as they sent, and you have
hurt him more than they have hurt you, and I would not have them
arrested, for it might cost you something, and I wouldn't like to see
you pay anything out, for I know they were in fault." This the officer
done, pulling the wool over my eyes, I not knowing at the time what it
was done for. When I came to find out, to my great surprise, they were
all Secesh Democrats, well-met fellows together. Therefore, reader, you
can see the result of appointing such men as peace officers. In a few days
afterwards I went to New York on some business. Whilst walking up
Battery street, I saw an office and a sign of broking and shipping, with a
great deal of gold and silver in the window. I went in and asked, saying,
"Mister, will you be kind enough to tell me where to go to buy a ticket
for California?" He answered, "I will sell you a ticket for California." I
asked, "Is this the regular ticket office for California?" He said, "Yes." He

asked if I belonged in California. I said, "Yes." He said, "I thought you was a stranger." At that time I had on a gold watch and chain. He stepped up to me, taking hold of the chain, saying, "What a pretty chain! Where did you get it?" I answered, "In California." He said that he would like to buy the chain. I told him that I would not sell the chain without the watch. He asked to see the watch. I let him see it, and he said, "I will buy them both. What will you take for them?" As I was all ready for a trade, I thought that I had struck a green hand, and thinking that I had a chance to make my passage clear, I put a price on of forty dollars more than the watch or chain cost me. He answered, "All right; that is cheap enough." And he wanted to take it out to see if it was gold, and if so he would buy it. He turned back and said, "Show me how to take off the chain; I want to weigh it, to see how much it weighs." I took the chain off and handed it to him. He said, "Give me the watch, too." I gave it to him. At the same time his partner called my attention, saying, "If we buy your watch you will buy a ticket of us," showing me the picture of a ship, and remarking, "What a pretty-built ship!" It was while I was speaking to him, his partner put a bogus watch on the chain, handing it to me, saying, "Your watch is only worth twenty shillings, but I will give you twenty-five dollars for the chain." I asked him if he thought I stole the watch. And as I went to put it in my pocket I noticed it was not my watch. I said, "Will you please, sir, to give me my watch; this is not my watch." He said, "That is your watch." I said, "It is not, sir." He said, "You had better say that I stole your watch." I said, "I don't say that, but this is not my watch." He said, "If you say that I stole it I will break your head." I went to some white gentlemen who knew my watch. They said, "This is the same chain, but this is not the watch that I have seen. You come with me, and we will get a detective after him." We did so and had him arrested. By the time I got to the office he had about twenty men, that I had never seen, to swear that the watch that he gave me was the same one that I showed him. I supposed them to be his associates, as they fell in, one by one, as we went to the office. There was so much whispering between the officers and the Judge to the prisoner, that I came to the conclusion that they were all looking through one telescope. The Judge said, "Mr. Williams, I will prosecute them. I will put them through, if you say so." Right before the prisoner I said, "No, sir; I see enough. If I fool here I will have no money to get home with." Out I walked, and the officer followed me out, saying, "Mr. Williams, I have arrested this man, and I want you to prosecute him." I said, "No, sir; do you suppose I am fool enough to swear against all of those men to have them outswear me, and no one to corroborate my statement, and bring me in for the costs?" And away I went to my boarding-house, taking my carpet-sack, and started for Philadelphia. When I got down to Fulton Market I met a very nice gentleman, looking like a rich merchant, and he said, "How do you do, sir? Can you tell me what time the boat starts?" I said, "I don't know, sir; I think about four o'clock, by what I have understood." He asked me which way I was going, East or West? I said, "I am going to Philadelphia." He said, "There is just where I am going. We have plenty of time. We have a half of an hour yet. Come and take a drink!" "Thank you, sir; I don't drink." At the same time a man came up behind me, and struck me on the back of the leg, and the man I was speaking to said: "There, that man has got your pocket-book." I said, "It is not mine." He said, "Just say so, and we will make some money out of it." Reader, I had heard of the drop-game. As I had just been fooled, I came to the conclusion to see it out. This nice gentleman that looked like a merchant, called out, "Say, sir, you have got this man's pocket-book. I saw you when you picked it up." The man said, "I found it down there, and if I give it up he will not give me anything for finding it." Then this nice gentleman said, "How much do you want for finding it?" He answered, "Twenty dollars," and pretended to be a-crying. This gentleman, taking out a greenback, saying to me, "Have you got any gold? Give him a ten-dollar gold-piece." I put my finger to my eye, and asked, "Do you see anything green?" And away I went aboard the boat for Philadelphia. June 3, 1870, I left Philadelphia, the fourth time, for California, and landed in Sacramento on the eleventh of the next month, and went to my legitimate business, whitewashing. I worked at that three or four weeks, when I was employed by the trustees of the Siloam Baptist Church, as an agent to collect money to pay off the indebtedness of that church. As a general thing, amongst the people of color in their churches, you can never do enough for them, or satisfy them; so, after collecting some seven or eight months, I resigned my office as a collector.

> Not unto us, Lord, not unto us,
> But unto Thy Name give glory,
> For Thy mercy and for Thy truth.
> I love the Lord, because he heard my voice.

After I resigned my office as a collector, I opened a store on J street, between Ninth and Tenth, for groceries, fruit and poultry. This was in 1871. Reader, observe closely as you read. A colored lady that I had been acquainted with in the Eastern States wanted me to assist her to come to California, and I did so. After she arrived in California, she asked me to loan her money, to assist her to bring her mother out, and I did so. After her mother arrived here, she asked me to lend her some money to furnish a house, and I also did that. She asked me to go to Mr. Wingate, and stand security for her house-rent. I did that. When the rent was due she did not have the money. Mr. Wingate called at my store, and I paid it. Whilst I remained her security, whenever he called I paid the bill. Whenever she wanted groceries, she came to my store, money or no money, and she got whatever she wanted. This lady and myself were the best of friends. I was in the habit of going to her house two or three times daily. She would go with me anywhere and everywhere, when I requested her, and would do anything for me that laid in her power.

I was there at her house one afternoon in February, 1872, and leaving at five o'clock to go home, she followed me to the door, and remarked that she felt unwell, and would like some lager beer, and I called a young man that was present at the house, and asked him if he would go, and get some beer for Lizey. I gave her ten cents, and she and Alfred Linchcomb went in the house, bidding me good-afternoon, as I supposed, to get the pitcher for the beer. I come down K street to Ninth street; my attention was drawn by two white gentlemen talking politics. After standing there awhile, the bell rang for six o'clock. I went to the Golden Eagle barber shop, and called Mr. Christopher, saying, "Are you going home to supper?" And we both went down Sixth street together. It was raining at that time. I raised my umbrella, and we went together as far as O street. I went to my house, and he went home. After arriving at home, I ate my supper, and a lady came in about seven o'clock, and we had a little fun. Afterwards I laid down on the lounge, and went to sleep, to the best of my knowledge. The lady of the house called me, about ten o'clock, to get up from the lounge and go to bed. This was a dark, rainy, stormy night. The lady of the house was sewing, and the house shook so by the wind that she had not gone to bed yet, being troubled with the cramp. About one or half-past one o'clock, I was aroused by her saying that some one was at the door, asking for Williams. I told her to ask what was wanted. The man said, "Tell Mr. Williams that Miss Thompson's house is burnt down." I asked, "What Miss Thompson?" He answered, "Your Miss Thompson, on Eighth street." I said, "Where is she?" He said that she was burnt, too. I said, "My God, you don't say so? Come in, until I get my clothes on." Then we went to Mr. Slaughter's, and called two other gentlemen, friends of Miss Thompson, to go with us to the house. Reader, take notice and observe closely as you read. That day, at the coroner's jury, there were several examined, and I among the rest, and there was nothing found against me. They asked me who was at the house. I answered that I left Alfred Linchcomb there. "Where is he now?" No one had seen him that day that was then present. An officer, accompanied by some colored men, went to find him, and when they brought Linchcomb in, the first thing that I noticed was that he had changed his pantaloons, and the second thing that I noticed was the rings on his fingers, that looked just like hers; the third thing I noticed was, he hung his head on the palm of his hand, and could not hold it up; the fourth thing I noticed, he said that Fred Washington was with him, and Fred Washington had gone to San Francisco the previous day, for I shook hands with him just as he went on the boat; the next thing I noticed, he said that there was a gentleman with him by the name of Smith, and the officers brought all the colored men they could find in the city, by the name of Smith. But when they came, none appeared to be the man. So you see there was a lie somewhere. My humble opinion and my belief is, that there was no one with him but the devil. The officers, seeing his guilt, arrested him. Then his colleagues and my enemies tried to throw it on me to clear him, more especially the low and degraded class of colored people, standing on the corners, and holding caucuses, trying to poison the minds of every well-known respectable white citizen. I was then arrested, and falsely imprisoned, slandered falsely by the newspapers throughout the State, and throughout the United States, and held fourteen days in jail in this manner, yet being innocent. I was not alarmed, for I trusted in God, as the three Hebrew children did in the fiery furnace. When I prayed, they said that I was hardening. I said that if the word of God was hardening, then they may be hardened by the word of God,

> Then well may I say, in the Garden of Eden
>   There was beauty.
> In the Garden of Eden Beauty woke
>   And spoke to Beauty.
> And from the word there was beauty.
> In the Garden of Eden Beauty became
>   A living mortal.

When it came to trial, there was nothing against me, and I was discharged, and could not receive any reward as damage for false imprisonment, when I had proved that I was home and in bed, and had not been out of the house that night. Reader, is that a just law, that a man should be arrested in that manner and held for fourteen days on suspicion? Away with such abominable law as that! I hope to see the day when some good, honest-hearted man will be elected to the Legislature, who will stand up and use all of his own force and endeavor to make laws that no innocent man shall be arrested and held over twenty-four hours on suspicion; and furthermore, he should not be published in the papers until he is known to be guilty, and if such things should be done, the State and County should be held liable for heavy damages. In February, 1872, I sold out my store. I went to work at the Central Pacific R. R. shops, whitewashing, and acting as foreman of the whitewashers. In August, whilst at my employment, I was arrested, charged with a crime that I knew nothing about—taken the second time, charged with the same crime that I was not guilty of, and placed in Chokee, in that low, dirty, cold, miserable place, where you are half starved and don't receive good attention by the keeper. I do not believe that they give you what rations the law allows you. I caught my death-cold there, for I have not had a well day since. Though I look healthy, I am far from it. I would have sued the State and County for damages if I could, but the authorities fell back on their dignity, and said, "We had a right to arrest him on suspicion."

Ah, reader, is that fair to hold a man fourteen days on suspicion, and, when proved innocent, he to receive no damages for it? I gave Officers Geo. Harvey, Moore and Rider credit for their respectful treatment of me. They did no more than their duty. They did not hatch up lies to convict an innocent man, as many others do. My opinion is that the poor men of the United States do not get justice at law as the rich man does. We should have the best laws in these United States of any place on the face of the globe, but we are far from it. England now is not as strong as the United States, and her laws are few, but more powerful than the laws of the United States. She protects her subjects at home and abroad, more especially at home. Now, reader, let us see the difference between the United States and England, relative to the poorer class of people. There was a white man brought from Idaho, supposed to be Weeks, the murderer, on suspicion. They kept him in about half of the time they kept Williams in Chokee. After he was proven not to be the man, oh, what did they do? I noticed that the people of this city raised him some four or five thousand dollars, and gave him a benefit in the theatre. What did you do for Williams, the poor negro? You did not even honorably acquit him through your papers. When some of you will be in torment, calling for water to cool your parched tongues, I expect to be in Abraham's bosom. I mean those who are my accusers. Then, when I was arraigned for general trial, what did the District Attorney say to the Judge? "Judge, your honor, I have no case, or no evidence, to show that this man is guilty. You have heard all the evidence in this case, and there is nothing against him. There was no evidence before the jury when they indicted him. Only the darkies made such a fuss, we thought that we had better hold him, to see if there could be anything found against him." So the District Attorney made a motion to dismiss the case. Now, reader, is that fair? Where are my damages for being falsely imprisoned? I am speaking against office-holders and office-seekers. All that I can receive for damages is for the people to buy my book. I am wounded and injured for life in my reputation; everybody looks down on me with a frowning, treacherous look, throughout the world, far and near, wherever I am known. Is it fair that a man should be browbeat in this manner without any cause? My heart is clear, my hands are clear, my mind is clear, my skirts are clear. I am as clear as the glittering sun of any blood-stain to my skirts. I never have harmed or injured any living thing on the face of the earth, not even to the beasts. I have always been kind-hearted, benevolent and good-natured to all races, colors and sexes, without any prejudice whatever. Reader, you can believe this or let it alone. It is immaterial to me whether you believe it or not. God is my sacred Judge. He is sufficient for all things. I will ever trust in Him. If He is for me, all hell may be against me, and cannot shake my foundation. "Oh," says one, "why is it that your own people are so down on you, or what did you do that they so dislike you?" I will tell you: I am a little Southern boy, born in the South, and never had any training at school, having more brains than some of the Northern boys have education. You ask the colored man what is my reputation? He will say, "He is a bad man." "Well, what did he do to you?" "O, nothing;" "Well, what did you know him to do?" "O, nothing; but they say he is a bad man." "How long have you known him?" "Ten or fifteen years; but they say he is a bad man—they say he is a sharper." "What kind of a sharper—a gambler?" "No; they say he is sharp, beats you in trade, and he fights." "Is that all?" "Yes, that is all." "Don't he work?" "Yes." Reader, these phrases are used by colored men that call themselves learned men. Where do you find them? In the whisky mills, the most intellectual colored men we have in our community—at the card table and the billiard tables. That is the class of men that have been browbeating the Southern boy. Are they a criterion to be ruled by or governed by? "Yes; they say your church brothers and sisters despise you. What did you do to them?" Let us examine ourselves closely, and see what we have done. One brother, Sheppard, spoke disorderly in the board meeting. I, doing my duty as a trustee, made a charge against him, and handed him over to the Quarterly Conference, and he was set back. Another brother I spoke to about his breath smelling of whisky in time of service. They always told me that they would get even with me, and this is their little grievance. "But they say he is a bad man; he robbed the church." Well, let us see how he robbed the church. They appointed him collector and agent for the church. They allowed me two dollars a day and traveling expenses, but I must make the money myself. I done so, and turned in about three thousand dollars in eight months, clear of all my expenses. This is what they call robbing the church. There was great confusion amongst the trustees all the time I was collecting, thinking that I was making an easy living. There was one brother amongst them that could shout higher than I could, and was fuller of the Holy Ghost than I was, or he pretended to be, and was very anxious for the office, and his friends were anxious for him to have it. After settling up at the trustees' meeting, and they saying that everything was satisfactory, they said that they would like to have the books, for they could send out a man that could turn in a little more money than I could in that time. They sent out one Mr. Johnson. He went to San Francisco. I am told that he collected three or four hundred dollars. The sight of the money did him so much good, that he went to keeping restaurant, and never came back. As far as I understand and know, he backslid from the church. When he used to be giving in his experience at the meeting, he used to say, "My name is John Johnson, bound for heaven." So, reader, you see these are the kind of men that rule the colored church. Ah, Williams robbed the church, did he? Let us inquire little further into it. Who did they send out next? One good old M. E. preacher, by the name of Elder Handy, who said that he would not deal with the trustees, and wanted the privilege of turning his money in at the General Conference at the end of the year. At the end of the year, he turned into Conference fifty dollars, and said that it took all that he could collect to pay his board and traveling expenses. So Williams is a bad man; they say he robbed the church. What do you think of this story? Reader, the worst enemies that I ever had in my life were men and women that belonged to the church. The A. M. church in California preach up a great deal of religion, but practice but little. You may visit the class-room of the A. M. church, and you will find three or four brothers and sisters all going to heaven, and one won't speak to the other, though they turned me out when I was present, without a legal notice, and they never have told me what I was turned out for. Is that Christianity? May the Lord forgive them, for they know not what they are doing. Let not our hearts be troubled, but live and fear the Lord, and trust in him forever. The whole world may be against me, but yet I will trust in the Lord. O, let us seek him with all our hearts, and by his power we will be borne up. Reader, they say Williams is a bad man. Yes, Linchcomb said that he done the deed. Why did he say so? Because he saw that there was no alternative to save himself. Then his friends and my enemies, after seeing that he was convicted, in order to take the stain off of his mother and kindred, said to him, "You just say that it is Williams, and that will keep the disgrace from us." Or, in other words, if public influence can saddle it on Williams, we perhaps can clear you, or, after a while, get you pardoned out. Reader, he could not come out until after he was convicted. What do you think of that for an innocent man? His friends tried hard to put up a job on me. They produced a hat, purporting it to be mine; but, thank God, it was four inches too small for me, and, furthermore, it was found three weeks before the circumstance happened. What do you think of such malice?

And they went so far as to try to persuade the lady with whom I was stopping to say that I was out when I was in; and said to her, if he had been stopping with you, I would say he was out anyhow. But she would not lie; and then they tried to make her run away. But she said, "What will I run away for? I have done nothing wrong, and I know nothing wrong of anybody else for me to run away." And they furthermore said to her, "We don't care who hangs or who don't as long as we clear Linchcomb." This was done by colored people. In my humble belief they are the most treacherous people in the city of Sacramento, State of California, or any portion of the world I ever traveled. Ah, my colored brethren were not aware of the joke we practiced on Linchcomb while in jail. I placed two officers behind his cell, went to the door, and the keeper said: "Mr. Linchcomb, Mr. Williams wants to see you," and he walked off and left me as he thought, the same time I having two officers placed behind the door. Says I, "Mr. Linchcomb, why don't you come out and tell the people that I have nothing to do with this, and not keep me locked up for nothing." And says he, "I will say nothing that will implicate myself, for my attorney has advised me what to do, and told me not to talk to any one." And he looks up at me, and says: "How is it that the keeper will allow you to come and talk by yourself, because they are very particular to come and listen when anybody else comes in." Ah, reader, if I was so guilty, as he stated after the conviction, why did he not state it at the cell-door when we were alone, or supposed to be?

Well may it be noted that "a drowning man will catch at a straw to save himself." Reader, you have heard of the cat story: Once upon a time two cats stole a cheese. After stealing it, they did not know how to divide it; they called in a monkey to divide it. He, making himself and believing himself to be the judge, opened Court, and called for the scales, and, breaking the cheese, placed each part in the scales; but one side weighing heavier than the other, he bit off a piece, and he said, "The other side is little the heavier," and he bit a piece off of it; and so he kept on biting. At last the cats got to grumbling, and said, "Give each of us our share, and we will go off satisfied," and says he, "No, I am the judge of the Court; my friends have got to be provided for, the cost of the Court have to be paid, and the judge has to have his salary." And then he rams the other end in his mouth and dismisses the Court.

"Well, writer, what do you mean by that story?" Reader, I will show you. Read slow, and observe and take notice of what you read. Mrs. Fair committed a crime wilfully, and all effort was made to clear her, by trial after trial, until she was cleared. Tip McLaughlin committed a crime wilfully. All effort was made to clear him. Juries disagreed and disagreed until he was brought in guilty. I am not an enemy of these parties, neither do I have any ill-feeling towards them. I only draw up these resolutions to illustrate this story, to show to the intelligent portion of the people the injustice of the law. I have seen more law in California than any other part of the world which I have traveled in, but, according to my belief, *little justice*. "Can you prove that?" I can, by relating the cat story, and referring to the Tip McLaughlin case. When the jury brought in a verdict of *guilty*, says the Court, "My friends and the Court are not satisfied. We will walk out and take a drink, and let him skedaddle." How did you treat poor Williams, the darky, who was not guilty of any crime? You kept him in close confinement, guarded by two strong officers, and the bloodhounds were running far and near, trying to implicate him, when there was nothing against him. So you see the difference. A man that is innocent they try to convict, and one that is guilty they let him walk out of the courthouse. Remember, if I am not educated, that I have good sound mother-wit, and take notice of the actions of office-holders. In comes the cat story again. After my money was gone they let me go, as the monkey did the cats, and rammed it all in his mouth, and dismissed the Court, and I went whining, as the cats did, about my most shameful treatment throughout the State of California. But be it known, that the Anglo-Saxon race were my best friends through it all.

A Few Sketches of the Catholic and
Protestant Churches.

The Protestants say that the Catholics worship idols. I want to show you that I am of a Methodist opinion and Methodist belief. I am going to show you, according to my weak opinion, that there is no difference in religion. Yes, but the Catholics bow down to wooden images. Is there anything wrong about that? They do it as a token of remembrance of Christ. Don't the Protestants have likenesses of some great man, or of their fathers or mothers, and worship them in some like manner? Then why not have the picture of our Saviour in our houses? He is more to us than all of them. Crosses and trials and persecutions are of the way to heaven; but let us endeavor to give God the glory, and yet will I trust in Him all the days of my life, until my change takes place.

As far as I could see in all my travels the Catholic priests are thoroughly educated. Then they are not fools. You say that they address their prayers to the Virgin Mary, to get her to intercede with Christ for them. Is there anything wrong about that? The Protestants pray to the Son to intercede with the Father; but the Catholics say mass and go to the priest to confess. What does the priest say? He tells them to do nothing wrong, but to go in peace and sin no more. Is there anything wrong about that? The Methodists and Baptists have class meetings, and they stand up before a man that they call a leader and confess to him, and he tells them to do no evil, and to go in peace and sin no more. Is there any difference between the two?

Seeing this, it occurs to my mind what is the use of so much caviling against the Catholics, for the Protestants are, more or less, continually slandering the Catholics. They remind me of Jeff. Davis' followers, when they fired on Fort Sumpter, and then cried, "Let us alone." Reader, you ask the reason of my making these remarks concerning the Catholics. These came under my notice during my life. We are all living together, and should be friendly with one another, and not despise each other.

The Protestants bit off their noses to spite their own faces, in the taxation of their own churches to get to tax the Catholics. They are able to pay their taxes, while some of the Protestants are hardly able to pay the tax that is assessed on them. They are the most benevolent body that we have amongst us. They take care of their members and their sick, and provide for their widows, as far as I can see, and understand that their faith and belief are the bulwarks of religion. If you belong to a secret society in California, and are in good standing, and should go to Europe, and find a body there of the same association as that which you are identified with here, after undergoing a strict examination and finding you to be in good standing in the former association, then, by your good works and having the password, you are admitted to that association. Then let us live in the faith, and die in the faith, for faith is the key that unlocks the gate of heaven. The God of heaven will not ask us whether we are Catholics, Baptists or Methodists. There are but two places—heaven and hell. We are all striving for the same place; then let us stop ridiculing one another. I, J. Williams, found that the Catholics, whilst I was collecting for the A. M. E. Church, were very benevolent. Every priest in the State gave me something, except two. Father Cotter gave me $20, and Father Gibney gave $10, and another priest in this city gave me $15. Every priest that I called on in San Francisco gave me a liberal contribution, except one; and also in Marysville the priest gave me, as also did the Catholic priest in Grass Valley. Mr. Senks, of Grass Valley, informed me that the priest gave him $50 for the A. M. E. Church of that place. Is that not a good act? Why do we cavil so much against the Catholics? Let us live in harmony one with the other whilst on this earth, and help each other their burdens to bear. After death we will all live in heaven together, if we are prepared for that place, or else in the horrible pit with the rich man Dives.

"Blessed are ye when men shall revile you and persecute you, and say all manner of evil against you falsely, for my sake. Rejoice, and be exceedingly glad, for great is your reward in heaven, for so persecuted they the prophets which were before you."

In 1871 I was employed to solicit aid to pay a debt on the Siloam Baptist Church, of Sacramento. I found it an unthankful job, as I generally found it in other churches. There was confusion and jars, as usual in such bodies. One could not do enough. It is true, reader, that I am a professor of religion; also, I must state the fact that it is not all that make the loudest professions that are the most exemplary Christians. In all churches that I have been connected with, I have always found two parties, one working against the other. That is the cause of the confusion. I was employed just before a trustee election, and the old Board of Trustees demanded the moneys that I collected, saying that they put me in, and I must hand over the moneys collected to them. The new Board of Trustees took exceptions at it, and they published that I was no longer a collector for the Siloam Baptist Church, without stating that I had resigned, and settled in an honorable manner. Then I made them republish me, stating that I had resigned honorably, and my accounts were correct. My making them make a statement of collections, caused some hard feelings, and made me not a few enemies. I was informed that one of the members made a statement in the church, and asked for assistance to raise money to fee a lawyer to defeat the enemy, whilst I was in prison; that the enemy had employed one of the best lawyers in the State, and by making these remarks, I supposed that they were alluding to me. This was after the report of the coroner's jury.

James Williams testified before the coroner's jury, in the Lizey Thompson homicide, that the watch and other jewelry of the deceased were oroide, and not valuable. Another colored man, who also gave evidence, and who manifested much feeling against Williams, testified the watch was gold, he thought, and of considerable value. A manufacturing jeweler of this city, who repaired it, states that it was a small oroide cylinder escapement, not worth, when new, more than $15 in greenbacks. When Williams was examined upon the charge of being accessory to the homicide, there was not a particle of evidence against him, and it now appears that he, and not the other witness, assigned the true value to the woman's jewelry. And Williams further testified that the woman had $19 or $20 in the Sacramento Savings Bank; but the other witnesses testified that she had $150, but when the undertaker, Mr. Camboie Williams, and the girl's mother went to the bank, they found $19.85 to her credit. Reader, you can draw your own conclusion, whether I have been treated right by the people of color, and more especially by the church members, or a portion of them. I would advise all persons, especially the young, to avoid, as much as possible, handling moneys belonging to a church, and more especially the African churches, for that has done me more harm than anything that I know of, for that race do not give one another credit for anything good done for the whole body. Said one of the members in connection with one of the Methodist brothers, "He robbed Aunt Susan." Let us see how he has robbed her. I wish for the reader to know the facts in this particular case. An old colored lady, by the name of Susan Neal, came from Alabama to California with her owners, and gained her freedom by coming to California, and afterwards married Charles Neal, who died, and left her in debt. Then there was a suit brought against her for his debts, or for a debt; and to liquidate the said debt, she went around and begged money of the people. Sometime after paying that debt, a certain lawyer and a judge said that it she could pay one debt, she could pay them for fees due them. So they commenced suits against her for their fees. The day the trial was to come off, I met her in the street, crying. I said to her, "What is the matter, Aunt Susan?" She answered, "What has always been the matter with me?—the same thing that has always been the matter with me is the matter with me now. The people down South have got all my labor, and I have come to California, and got free, and made a little money, and now the white folks are trying to rob me out of that. There is a suit coming off to-day against me, and I have been to two or three colored men," calling their names, "asking them if they would help me, but just as soon as they found that they had a little money to pay, they would not do anything for me. I went to the society that my husband belonged to, the United Sons of Friendship, and said to them, 'If you will pay the debt on my property, and let me have it as long as I live, and then you can have it.' But when they found out that they had some money to pay out, they refused." Then she spoke to me and asked me if I would go and see her out to-day. I said, "Certainly," and I went with her to W. R. Cantwell's office, and settled the claim that he had against her, and didn't ask for any security. A few days afterwards, she came to me and said, "Mr. Williams, if you will pay off all the debts against my property, and protect me so that the white folks won't rob me any more, then, at my death, you can have it all, for I have no one in the world to care for me." Then she asked me to go with her to a lawyer. I went with her, and her lawyer explained it to her, and asked her if she knew what she was doing. She answered, "Yes, I know thoroughly what I am doing. I want to put my property in Mr. Williams' hands, so that the white folks can't rob me, and have him for a protector." He drew up the writings for her, and there was a white friend present throughout the transaction. Then, afterwards her lawyer explained the writing to her agent. Then we went to Judge Cross's office, and he read the papers and explained them to her, and she acknowledged them and seemed to be satisfied with their contents.

"Ah, Williams is a rascal," they say; "he robbed Aunt Sue out of her property." Now, reader, you can see how he robbed her. This is a true statement of the facts. Whilst I was doing this, no one had anything to say, one way or the other, either for or against, but just as soon as she got sick (I was in San Francisco at the time,) some of my enemies went to see her, and persuaded her to make a will in favor of some outside person that had never done anything for her, without regard to the deed that she had given to me. She being sick did not understand what she was doing, and in consequence of their importunities, she made the will, and when I came back, these parties that were with her would shut the door in my face, and refused to let me see her, and the groceries and provisions that I sent to her they would send back. Then, after her death, which happened about six weeks after the above occurrence, my enemies got themselves appointed to carry out the provisions of the will, and settled up the estate, and their services were given in, as they wished to assist the widow that the will was made in favor of; but afterwards, in settling up the estate, they demanded one hundred dollars for their services. When I found that they all wanted the property more than I did, I offered to compromise with them by their paying me the moneys that I had paid out, with interest. They did so, and set a trap to rob me out of about half the money, and succeeded in it. So you see how I robbed her. May God have mercy on such a sinful and treacherous set.

THE STORY OF CHARLES THOMPSON.

He was a member of the Baptist Church of Richmond. In stature he was medium size, color dark, hair long and bushy, rather of rawboned and rugged appearance, modest and self-possessed, with much more intelligence than would be supposed from first observation. On his arrival here, he had shaken hands with the British Lion's paw, which he was desirous of doing, and changed the habiliments in which he escaped. Having listened to the recital of this thrilling tale, and wished to get it, we here produce it, word for word, as it flowed naturally from his lips. "How old are you?" "Thirty-two years first day of last June." "Were you born a slave?" "Yes." "How have you been treated?" "Badly, all of the time, for the last twelve years." "What do you mean by being treated badly?" "I have been whipped, and they never gave me anything." "What was the name of your master?" "Fleming Bibbs." "Where did you live?" "In Caroline County, fifty miles above Richmond." "What did your master do?" "He was a farmer." "Did you ever live with him?" "I never did. He always hired me out, and then I couldn't please him." "What kind of a man was he?" "A man with a very severe temper, would drink at all times, though he would do it slily." "Was he a member of any church?" "Yes, a Baptist; he would curse at his servants, as if he weren't in any church." "Was his family members of the church, too?" "Yes." "What kind of family had he?" "His wife was a tolerable fair woman, but his sons were dissipated, and all of them rowdies and gamblers. The sons have had children by the servants. One of his daughters had a child by his grandson last April. They are traders—buy and sell." "How many slaves did he own?" "Fifteen besides myself." "Did any of them know that you were going to leave?" "No; I saw my brother on Tuesday, but never said a word to him about it." "What put it in your head to leave?" "It was bad treatment for being put in jail for soil, the 7th day of last January. I was whipped in jail, and after I came out the only thing they told me was that I had been selling newspapers about the street, and was half free." "Where did you live then?" "In Richmond. I have been living out for twenty-one years." "How much did your master receive a year for your services?" "From sixty-five to one hundred and fifty dollars." "Did you have to find yourself?" "No; the people who hired me found me. The general rule in Richmond is 75 cents for a week's board is allowed, and if a man gets any more than that he has to find it himself." "How about Sunday clothing?" "Find them yourself." "How about a house to live in?" "Have that to find yourself, and if you have a wife and family it makes no difference—they don't allow anything for that at all." "Suppose you are sick, who pays the doctor?" "Our master pays that." "How do you manage to make a little extra money?" "By getting up before day and carrying out papers, and doing other jobs, cleaning up single men's rooms and the like." "What have you been employed at in Richmond?" "Been working in a tobacco factory; this year I was hired to a printing office, the *National American*. I carried papers." "Had you a wife?" "I had, but her master was a very bad man, and was opposed to me, and would not let me come there to see my wife, and he persuaded her to take another husband, and being in his hands she took his advice." "How long ago was that?" "Near twelve months ago. She got married last fall." "Had you any children?" "Yes, five." "Where are they?" "Three are with Jacob Luck, her master; one with his sister, and the other belongs to Judge Hudgins, of Bowling Green." "Do you expect to see them again?" "No, not till the day of the great I Am." "What do you think of slavery?" "I think that it is a great curse, and I think the Baptists in Richmond will go to the deepest hell, if there is any, for they are so wicked they will work you all day and part of the night, and wear cloaks and long faces, and try to get all of the work out of you that they can, by telling you of Jesus Christ. Out of their extra money they have to pay a white man five hundred dollars a year for preaching." "What kind of preaching does he give you?" "He tells them if they die in their sins they will go to hell, and that they must obey their masters and mistresses; for good servants make good masters. All they want you to know is enough to say master and mistress, and run like lightning when they speak to you, and do just what they want you to do."

HENRY BOX BROWN.

Although the name of Henry Box Brown has been echoed over the land for a number of years, and the simple facts connected with his miraculous escape in a box from slavery published widely through the medium of anti-slavery papers, nevertheless, it is not unreasonable to suppose that very little is know in relation to his case. Brown was a man of invention as well as a hero. He was decidedly an unhappy piece of property in the City of Richmond, in the condition of a slave. He felt that it would be impossible for him to remain. Full well did he know that it was no holiday task to escape the vigilance of Virginia slave-hunters, as the wrath of an enraged master, for committing the unpardonable sin of attempting to escape to a land of liberty, would be unappeasable. So Brown counted well the cost before venturing upon his hazardous undertaking. Ordinary modes of travel, he concluded, might prove disastrous to his hopes. He, therefore, hit upon a new invention, which was to have himself boxed up and forwarded to Philadelphia, direct, by express. The size of the box and how it was to be made to fit him most comfortably was of his own ordering. Two feet eight inches deep, two feet wide, and three feet long, was the exact dimensions of the box lined with baize. His resources, with regard to food and water, consisted of one bladder of water and a few small biscuit. Satisfied that it would be far better to peril his life for freedom in this way than to remain under the galling yoke of slavery, he entered his box, which was safely nailed up, and hooped with five hickory hoops, and was then addressed by his next friend, James A. Smith, a shoe dealer, to Wm. H. Johnson, Arch street, Philadelphia, marked "This side up with care." In this condition he was sent to Adams' Express office, in a dray, and thence by overland express to Philadelphia. It was twenty-six hours from the time he left Richmond until his arrival in the City of Brotherly Love. The notice, "This side up with care," did not avail much; for awhile they actually had the box upside down, and had him standing on his head, for miles. A few days before he was expected, certain intimation was conveyed to a member of the Vigilance Committee, that a box might be expected by the three o'clock morning train from the South, which might contain a man. One of the most serious walks he ever took, was at half-past two o'clock that morning, to the depot—not once, but for more than a score of times. He fancied the slave would be dead. He anxiously looked while the freight was being unloaded from the cars, to see if he could recognize a box that might contain a man. One alone had that appearance, and he confessed it really seemed as if there was a scent of death about it. But, on inquiry, he soon learned that it was not the one he was looking for. That same afternoon he received from Richmond a telegram, which read thus: "Your case of goods is shipped, and will arrive to-morrow morning." At this exciting juncture of affairs, Mr. McKim, who had been engineering this important undertaking, deemed it expedient to change the programme slightly, in one particular, at least, to insure greater safety. Instead of having a member of the Committee go again to the depot for the box, which might excite suspicion, it was decided that it would be safest to have the express bring it direct to the Anti-Slavery office. But all apprehensions of danger did not now disappear, for there was no room to suppose that Adams' Express office had any sympathy with the abolitionists or the fugitive; consequently, it was contemplated that Mr. McKim should appear personally at the Express office to give directions with reference to the coming of a box from Richmond, which would be directed to Arch street, and yet not intended for that street, but for the Anti-Slavery office, at 107 North Fifth street. It needed, of course, no great discernment to foresee that a step of this kind would be wholly impracticable, and that a more indirect and covert method would have to be adopted in this dreadful crisis. Mr. McKim, with his usual good judgment and remarkable quick strategetical mind, especially in matters pertaining to the U. G. Railroad, hit upon the following plan, namely, to go to his friend, E. M. Davis, who was engaged in mercantile business, and relate the circumstances. Having daily intercourse with the said office, and being well acquainted with the firm and some of the drivers, Mr. Davis could, as Mr. McKim thought, talk about boxes, freight, etc., from any part of the country, without risk.

Mr. Davis heard Mr. McKim's plan, and instantly approved of it, and was heartily at his service. "Dan, an Irishman, one of Adams' Express drivers, is just the fellow to go to the depot after the box," said Davis. "He drinks a little too much whisky sometimes, but he will do anything I ask him to do promptly. I'll trust Dan, for I believe him to be the very man." The difficulty which Mr. McKim had been so anxious to overcome, was thus pretty well settled. It was agreed that Dan should go after the box next morning, before daylight, and bring it to the Anti-Slavery office, and to make it all the more agreeable for Dan to get up out of his warm bed and go on this errand before day, it was decided that he should have a five-dollar gold piece for himself. Thus these preliminaries having been satisfactorily arranged, it only remained for Mr. Davis to see Dan, and give him instructions accordingly.

Next morning, according to arrangement, the box was at the Anti-Slavery office in due time. The witnesses present to behold the resurrection were: J. McKim, C. D. Cleaveland, L. Thompson, and the writer. All was quiet. The door had been safely locked. The proceedings commenced, Mr. McKim stepped quietly on the lid of the box, and called out, "All right." Instantly came the answer from within, "All right, sir." The witnesses will never forget that moment. Saw and hatchet quickly had the five hickory hoops cut and the lid off, and the marvelous resurrection of Brown ensued. Rising up in his box, he reached out his hand, saying, "How do you do, gentlemen?" The little assemblage hardly knew what to think or do at the moment. He was as wet as if he come out of the Delaware River.

Very soon he remarked that, before leaving Richmond, he had selected to sing on his arrival, if he lived, the Psalm beginning with these words: "I waited patiently for the Lord, and he heard my prayer." And most touchingly did he sing the Psalm, much to his own relief as well as to the delight of his small audience. He was then christened "Henry Box Brown," and was soon afterwards sent to the hospitable residence of James Mott and E. M. Davis, on Ninth street, where, it is needless to say, he met a most cordial welcome from Mrs. Lucretia Mott and her household—clothing and creature comforts were furnished in abundance, and delight and joy filled all hearts. He had been so long doubled up in the box, he needed to promenade considerably in the fresh air. So James Mott put one of his broad-brim hats on his head, and tendered him the hospitalities of his yard as well as his house, whilst Brown promenaded the yard, flushed with victory. Great was the joy of his friends. After his visit at Mrs. Mott's, he spent two days with the writer, and then took his departure for Boston, evidently feeling quite conscious of the wonderful feat he had performed.

STORY OF A YOUNG WOMAN'S ESCAPE FROM SLAVERY
IN A BOX—NAME UNKNOWN.

In the winter of 1857, a young woman, who had just turned her majority, was boxed up in Baltimore by one who stood to her in the relation of a companion, a young man, who had the box conveyed as freight to the depot in Baltimore, consigned to Philadelphia. Nearly all one night it remained at the depot with the living agony in it, and, after being upside down more than once, the next day, about ten o'clock, it reached Philadelphia. Her companion, coming on in advance of the box, arranged with a hackman, George Custis, to attend to having it brought from the depot to a designated house, Mrs. Myers', 412 South Seventh street, where the resurrection was to take place. Curtis, without knowing exactly what the box contained, but suspected, from the apparent anxiety and instruction of the young man who engaged him to go after it. Whilst the freight car still stood in the street he demanded it of the freight agent, not willing to wait the usual time for delivery of freight. At first the freight agent declined delivering under such circumstances. The hackman insisted, by saying that he wished to dispatch it in great haste. "It is all right; you know me; I have been coming here for many years, every day, and will be responsible for it." The freight-master told him to take it and go ahead with it. No sooner said than done. It was placed in a one-horse wagon, at the instance of Custis, and driven to Seventh and Minster streets. The secret had been entrusted to Mrs. Myers by the young companion of the woman. A feeling of horror came over the aged woman who had been thus suddenly entrusted with such responsibility. A few doors from her lived an old friend of the same religious faith with herself, well known as a brave woman and a friend of the slave, Mrs. Ash, the undertaker, or shrouder, whom everybody knew among the colored people. Mrs. Myers thought it would not be wise to move in the matter of this resurrection without the presence of the undertaker. Accordingly she called for Mrs. Ash. Even her own family were excluded from witnessing the scene. The two aged women chose to be alone in that fearful moment, shuddering at the thought that a corpse might meet their gaze instead of a living creature. However, they mustered courage and pried off the lid. A woman was discovered in the straw, but no signs of life were perceptible. Their fears seemed fulfilled. Surely she is dead, thought the witnesses. "Get up, my child," spoke one of the women. With scarcely life enough to move the straw covering, she nevertheless did now show signs of life, but to a very faint degree. She could not speak, but, being assisted, arose. She was straightway aided up stairs, not yet uttering a word. After a short while she said: "I feel so deadly faint." She was then asked if she would not have some water or nourishment, which she declined. Before a great while, however, she was prevailed upon to take a cup of tea. She then went to bed, and there remained all day, speaking but a very little during that time. The second day she gained strength, and was able to talk much better, but not with ease. The third day she began to come to herself, and to talk quite freely. She tried to describe her sufferings and fears while in the box, but in vain. In the midst of her severest agonies, her chief fear was that she would be discovered and carried back to slavery. She had a pair of scissors with her, and, in order to procure fresh air, she had made a hole in the box, but it was very slight. How she ever managed to breathe and maintain her existence, being in the condition to become a mother, it was hard to comprehend. In this instance, the utmost endurance was put to test. She was obviously nearer death than Henry Box Brown, or any other of the box cases that ever came under the notice of the committee. In Baltimore she belonged to a wealthy and fashionable family, and had been a seamstress and ladies' servant generally. On one occasion, when sent of an errand for certain articles, in order to complete arrangements for the grand opening ball at the Academy of Music, she took occasion not to return, but was among the missing. Great search was made, and a large reward offered, but all to no purpose. A free colored woman who washed for the family was suspected of knowing something of her going, but they failing to get aught out of her, she was discharged. Soon after the arrival of this traveler at Mrs. Myers', the committee was sent for, and learned the facts as above stated. After spending some three days with Mrs. Myers' family, she was forwarded to Canada.

STORY OF HARRY GRIMES.

Harry was about forty-six years of age, according to his reckoning, full six feet high, and in muscular appearance very rugged, and in his countenance were evident marks of firmness. He was born a slave in North Carolina, and had been sold three times. The first time when a child, second time when he was thirteen, and the third and last time to Jesse Moore, from whom he fled. He said that he had been treated very bad. One day we were grubbing, and master said we didn't do work enough. "How come it there was no more work done that day?" said master to me. I told him I did work. In a more stormy manner he repeated the question. I then spoke up, and said: "Massa, I don't know what to say." At once master plunged his knife into my neck, causing me to stagger. He was drunk. He then drove me down to the black folks' cabins. He then got his gun, and called the overseer, and told him to get some ropes. While he was gone, I said, "Master, now you are going to tie me up and cut me all to pieces for nothing." In a great rage he said, "Go!" I jumped, and he put up his gun and snapped both barrels at me. He then set his dogs on me, but as I had been in the habit of making much of them, feeding them, they would not follow me. I kept on straight to the woods. My master and overseer caught the horses and tried to run me down, but as the dogs would not follow me, they could not make anything of it. It was the last of August, one year ago; the devil was into him, and he flogged and beat four of the slaves, one man and three of the women, and said, if he could only get hold of me he wouldn't strike me nary a lick, but would tie me to a tree and empty both barrels into me. My master was a man about fifty years of age, a right red-looking man, a big bellied old fellow; weighed about two hundred and forty pounds; he drank hard; he was just like a rattlesnake, and so cross and crabbed when he spoke, seemed like he could go through you. He flogged a slave, called Richmond, for not plowing the corn good. That was what he pretended to whip him for. Richmond ran away—was gone four months, as nigh as I can guess. Then they caught him, then struck him a hundred lashes, and then they split both feet to the bone, and split both his insteps, and then master took his knife and stuck it into him in many places. After he had done him in that way, he put him in the barn to shucking corn. For a long time he was not able to work. When he did partly recover, he was set to work again.

When I was in the woods, I lived on nothing, you may say, and yet something, too. I had bread, and roasting ears, and potatoes. I stayed in the hollow of a big tree for seven months. The other part of the time I stayed in a cave. I suffered mighty bad with the cold, and for the want of something to eat. Once I got me some charcoal, and made me a fire in my tree to warm myself, and it like to have killed me. So I had to take the fire out. One time a snake came and poked its head in the hollow, and was coming in, and I took my axe and chopped him in two. It was a poplar-leaf moccasin, the poisonest kind of a snake we have. While in the woods, all of my thoughts were how to get away to a free country.

Subsequently, in going back over his past history, he referred to the fact that, on an occasion long before the cave and tree existence, already noticed, when suffering under this brutal master, he sought protection in the woods, and abode twenty-seven months in a cave, before he surrendered himself or was captured. His offence, in this instance, was simply because he desired to see his wife, and stole away from his master's plantation, and went a distance of five miles to where she lived, to see her. For this grave crime, his master threatened to give him a hundred lashes and to shoot him. In order to avoid this punishment, he escaped to the woods. The lapse of a dozen years, and recent struggles for existence, made him think lightly of his former troubles, and he would doubtless have failed to recall his earlier conflicts. He was asked if he had a family. "Yes, sir," he answered, "I had a wife and eight children, belonging to the Widow Slade." Harry gave the names of his wife and children: wife named Susan, children named Olive, Sabey, Washington, Daniel, Jonas, Harriet, Moses, Rosetta; the last-named he had never seen. Between my mistress and my master there was not much difference.

Story of George Laws, of Delaware.

George represented the ordinary young slave-men of Delaware. He was of unmixed blood, medium size, and of humble appearance. He was destitute of the knowledge of spelling, to say nothing of reading. Slavery had stamped him unmistakably for life, to be scantily fed and clothed, and compelled to work without hire. George did not admire that, but had to submit without murmuring. Indeed, he knew that his so-called master, whose name was Denny, would not be likely to heed complaints from a slave. He, therefore, dragged his chains, and yielded to his daily task.

One day, while hauling dirt with a fractious horse, the animal manifested an unwillingness to perform his duty satisfactorily. At this procedure, the master charged George with provoking the beast to do wickedly, and in a rage he collared George, and bade him accompany him up the stairs of the soap-house. Not daring to resist, George went along with him. Ropes being tied around both his wrists, the block and tackle were fastened thereto, and George soon found himself hoisted on tiptoe, with his feet almost clear of the floor. The kind-hearted master then tore all the poor fellow's old shirt off his back, and addressed him thus: "You son of a b—h, I will give you, pouting around me. Stay there till I go up town for my cowhide." George begged piteously, but in vain. The fracas caused some excitement, and it so happened that a show was exhibited that day in the town, which, as is usual in the country, brought a great many people from a distance. So, to his surprise, when the master returned with his cowhide, he found that a large number of curiosity-seekers had been attracted to the soap-house to see Mr. Denny perform with his cowhide on George's back, as he was stretched up by his hands. Many had evidently made up their minds that it would be more amusing to see the cowhiding than the circus. The spectators numbered about three hundred. This was a larger number than Mr. Denny had been accustomed to perform before, consequently he was seized with embarrassment. Looking confused, he left the soap-house, and went to his office to await the dispersion of the crowd. The throng finally retired, and left George hanging in mortal agony. Human nature here made a death-struggle. The cords which bound his wrists were unloosed, and George was then prepared to strike for freedom, at the mouth of the cannon or at the point of the bayonet. How Denny regarded the matter, when he found that George had not only cheated him out of the anticipated delight of cowhiding him, but had also cheated him out of himself, is left for the imagination to picture.

PETER MATHEWS, ALIAS SAMUEL SPARROW.

Up to the age of thirty-five, Pete had worn the yoke steadily, if not patiently, under William S. Mathews, of Oak Hall, near Temperanceville, in the State of Virginia. Pete said that his master was not a hard man, but the man to whom he was hired, George Mathews, was a very cruel man. "I might as well be in the penitentiary as in his hands," was his declaration one day. A short while before, Pete took out an ox, which had broke into the truck-patch and helped himself to choice delicacies, to the full extent of his capacious stomach, making sad havoc with the vegetables generally. Peter's attention being directed to the ox, he turned him out and gave him what he considered proper chastisement. According to the mischief done at this liberty taken by Pete, the master became furious. He got his gun and threatened to shoot him. "Open your mouth if you dare, and I will put the whole load in you," said the enraged master. "He took out a large dirk-knife, and attempted to stab me, but I kept out of his way," said Pete. Nevertheless, the violence of the master did not abate until he had beaten Pete over the head and body until he was very weary with inflicting severe injuries. A great change was at once wrought into Pete's mind. He was now ready to adopt any plan that might hold out the least encouragement to escape. Having capital to the amount of four dollars only, he felt that he could not do much towards employing a conductor, but he had a good pair of legs, and a heart stout enough to whip two or three slave-catchers with the help of a pistol. Happening to know who had a pistol for sale, he went to him and told him that he wished to purchase it for one dollar. The pistol became Pete's property. He had but three dollars left, but he was determined to make that amount answer his purposes, under the circumstances. The last cruel beating maddened him almost to desperation, especially when he remembered how he had been compelled to work hard night and day, under Mathews. Then, too, Peter had a wife, whom his master prevented him from visiting. This was not among the least offences with which Pete charged his master. Fully bent on leaving, the following Sunday was fixed by him on which to commence his journey.

The time arrived, and Pete bade farewell to slavery, resolved to follow the North Star, with his pistol in hand, ready for action. After traveling about two hundred miles from home, he unexpectedly had an opportunity of using his pistol. To his astonishment, he suddenly came face to face with a former master, whom he had not seen for a long time. Peter desired no friendly intercourse with him whatever, but he perceived that his old master recognized him, and was bent on stopping him. Pete held on to his pistol, but moved, as fast as his wearied limbs would allow him, in an opposite direction. As he was running, Pete cautiously cast his eye over his shoulder, to see what had become of his old master, when, to his amazement, he found that a regular chase was being made after him. The necessity of redoubling his pace was quite obvious in this hour of peril. Pete's legs saved him. After this signal leg-victory, Pete had more confidence in his understanding than he had in his old pistol, although he held on to it until he reached Philadelphia, where he left it in possession of the secretary of the Committee of the Underground Railroad. Pete was christened Samuel Sparrow. Mr. Sparrow had the rust of Slavery washed off as clean as possible, and the Committee, furnishing him with clean clothes, a ticket, and a letter of introduction, started him on to Canada, looking quite respectable. The unpleasantness which grew out of the mischief done by the ox on George Mathews' farm, took place the first of October, 1833.

Story of Leah Green.

Leah Green, so particularly advertised in the Baltimore *Sun* by James Noble, won for herself a strong claim to a high place among the heroic women of the nineteenth century. In regard to description and age the advertisement is tolerably accurate, although her master might have added that her countenance was one of peculiar modesty and grace, instead of saying she was of a dark brown color. Of her bondage, she made the following statement: She was owned by James Noble, a butter dealer of Baltimore. He fell heir to Leah by the will of his wife's mother, Mrs. Rachel Howard, by whom she had been previously owned. Leah was but a mere child when she came into the hands of Noble's family. She, therefore, remembered but little of her old mistress. Her young mistress, however, had made a lasting impression on her mind, for she was very exacting and oppressive in regard to the tasks she was daily in the habit of laying on Leah's shoulders, with no disposition whatever to allow her any liberties. At least, Leah was never indulged in this respect. In this situation, a young man, by the name of William Adams, proposed marriage to her. This offer she was inclined to accept, but disliked the idea of being encumbered with the chains of slavery and the duties of a family at the same time. After a full consultation with her mother, and also her intended, upon the matter, she decided that she must be free in order to fill the station of a wife and mother. For a time dangers and difficulties in the way of escape seemed utterly to set at defiance all hope of success. Whilst every pulse was beating strong for liberty, only one chance seemed to be left. The trial required as much courage as it would to endure the cutting off of the right arm or plucking out the right eye. An old chest, of substantial make, such as sailors commonly use, was procured. A quilt, a pillow, and a few articles of raiment, together with a small quantity of food and a bottle of water were put in it, and Leah placed therein. Strong ropes were fastened around the chest, and she was safely stowed amongst the ordinary freight, on one of the Erricson line of steamers. Her interested mother, who was a free woman, agreed to come as a passenger on the same boat. How could she refuse? The prescribed rules of the company assigned colored passengers to the deck. In this instance, it was exactly where this guardian and mother desired to be—as near the chest as possible. Once or twice, during the silent watches of the night, she was drawn irresistibly to the chest, and could not refrain from venturing to untie the rope and raise the lid a little, to see if the poor child lived, and, at the same time, to give her a breath of fresh air. Without uttering a whisper at that frightful moment, this office was successfully performed. That the silent prayers of this oppressed young woman, together with her faithful protector, were momentarily ascending to the ear of the good God above, there can be no doubt. Nor is it to be doubted for a moment but that some ministering angel aided the mother to unfasten the rope, and at the same time, nerved the heart of poor Leah to endure the trying ordeal of her perilous situation. She declared that she had no fear after she had passed eighteen hours in the chest. The steamer arrived at the wharf in Philadelphia, and, in due time, the living freight was brought off the boat, and at first was delivered at a house in Barley street, occupied by particular friends of the mother. Subsequently, chest and freight were removed to the residence of a friend, in whose family she remained several days, under the protection and care of the Vigilance Committee.

Such hungering and thirsting for liberty as was evinced by Leah Green, made the efforts of the most ardent, who were in the habit of aiding fugitives, seem feeble in the extreme. Of all the heroes in Canada, or out of it, who have purchased their liberty by downright bravery, through perils the most hazardous, none deserve more praise than Leah Green.

She remained for a time in this family and was then forwarded to Elmira. In this place she was married to William Adams, who has been previously alluded to. They never went to Canada, but took up their permanent abode in Elmira. The brief space of about three years only was allotted her in which to enjoy her freedom, as death came and terminated her career. The impressions made by both mother and daughter can never be effaced. The chest in which Leah escaped has been preserved by the writer, as a rare trophy, and her photograph, taken while in the chest, is an excellent likeness of her, and, at the same time, a fitting memorial.

LIBERTY; OR JIM BOW-LEGS.

In 1855 a trader arrived with the above name, who, on examination, was found to possess very extraordinary characteristics. As a hero and adventurer, some passages of his history were most remarkable. His schooling had been such as could only be gathered on plantations under brutal overseers, or while fleeing, or in swamps, in prisons, or on the auction-block, in which condition he was often found. Nevertheless, in these circumstances, his mind got well stored with vigorous thoughts, neither books nor friendly advisers being at his command, yet his native intelligence, as it regarded human nature, was extraordinary. His resolution and perseverance never faltered. In all respects he was a remarkable man. He was a young man, weighing about 180 pounds, of uncommon muscular strength. He was born in the State of Georgia, Oglethorpe county, and was owned by Dr. Thomas Stephens, of Lexington. On reaching the Vigilance Committee in Philadelphia his story was told, many times over, to one and another. Taking all of the facts into consideration respecting the courageous career of this successful adventurer for freedom, his case is by far more interesting than any that I have yet referred to. Indeed, for the good of the cause, and the honor of one who gained his liberty by periling his life so frequently, being shot several times, making six unsuccessful attempts to escape from the South, numberless times chased by bloodhounds, captured, sold and imprisoned repeatedly, living for months in the woods, swamps, and caves, subsisting mainly on parched corn and berries. His narrative ought, by all means, to be published, though I doubt very much whether many could be found who could persuade themselves to believe one-tenth part of this story.

His master, finding him not available on account of his absconding propensities, would gladly have offered him for sale. He was once taken to Florida for that purpose, but, generally, traders being wide awake, on inspecting him, would almost invariably pronounce him a damn rascal, because he would never fail to eye them sternly as they inspected him. The obedient and submissive slave is always recognized by hanging his head, and looking on the ground when looked at by a slaveholder. This lesson Jim Hall never learned. Hence he was not trusted. His head and chest, and, indeed, his entire structure, as solid as a rock, indicated that, physically, he was no ordinary man, and not being under the influence of non-resistance, he had occasionally been found to be rather a formidable customer. His father was a full-blooded Indian, brother to the noted Chief, Billy Bow-Legs. His mother was quite black, and of unmixed blood. For five or six years, the greater part of Jim's time was occupied in trying to escape, and being in prison, and for sale, to punish him for running away.

His mechanical genius was excellent, so was his geographical abilities. He could make shoes, or do carpenter work handily, though he had never had a chance to learn. As to traveling by night or day, he was always road-ready, and having an uncommon memory, could give exceedingly good accounts of what he saw. When he entered a swamp, and had occasion to take a nap, he took care, first, to decide upon the posture he must take, so that, if come upon unexpectedly by the hounds and slave-hunters, he might know, in an instant, which way to steer to defeat them. He always carried a liquid which he had prepared to prevent hounds from scenting him, which he said had never failed him. As soon as the hounds came on to the spot where he had rubbed his legs and feet with said liquid, they could follow him no further, but howled and turned immediately. A large number of friends of the slave saw this man, and would sit long and listen with the most undivided attention to his narrative, none doubting for a moment its entire truthfulness. Strange as this story was, there was so much natural simplicity in his manners and countenance, one could not refrain from believing him.

Abram Galoway and Richard Easler.

The Philadelphia branch of the U. G. R. R. was not fortunate in having very frequent arrivals from North Carolina, for such of her slaves as were sensible enough to travel north, found out nearer and safer routes than through Pennsylvania. Nevertheless, the Vigilance Committee had the pleasure of receiving some heroes who were worthy to be classed among the bravest of the brave. No matter who they may be who have claims to this distinction, in proof of this bold assertion, the two individuals whose names stand at the beginning of this article are presented. Abram was only twenty-one years of age, mulatto, five feet six inches in height, intelligent, and a perfect picture of good health. "What was your master's name?" "Milton Hawkins," answered Abram. "What business did he follow?" "He was chief engineer on the Wilmington Railroad; not a branch of the U. G. R. R.," responded Abram. "Describe him," said the members. "He was a slim-built, tall man, with whiskers; he was a man of very good disposition. I always belonged to him. He owned three slaves. He always said that he would sell before he would use a whip. His wife was a very mean woman. She would whip contrary to his orders." "Who was your father?" was further inquired. "John W. Galoway." "Describe your father." "He was captain of a government vessel. He recognized me as his son, and protected me as far as he was allowed so to do. He lived at Smithville, North Carolina. Abram's master, Milton Hawkins, lived at Wilmington, N. C." "What prompted you to escape?" was next asked. "Because times were hard, and I could not come up with my wages as I was required to do. So I thought I would try and do better." At this juncture Abram explained in what sense times were hard. In the first place, he was not allowed to own himself; he, however, prospered, hiring his time to service in the usual way. This favor was granted Abram, but he was compelled to pay $15 per month for his time, besides finding himself in clothing, food, paying doctor's bill, and per year head-tax.

Even under this master, who was a man of very good disposition, Abram was not contented. In the second place, he always thought slavery was wrong, although he had never suffered any personal abuse—toiling month after month, the year round, for the support of his master, and not himself, was the one intolerable thought.

Abram and Richard were intimate friends, and lived near each other. Being similarly situated, they could venture to communicate the secret feelings of their hearts to each other. Richard was four years older than Abram, with not so much Anglo-Saxon blood in his veins, but was equally as intelligent, and was by trade a fashionable barber, well known to the ladies and gentlemen of Wilmington. Richard owed service to Mrs. Mary Learen, a widow; she was very kind and tender to all of her slaves. "If I was sick," said Richard, "she would treat me the same way that my mother would." She was the owner of twenty men, women, and children, who were all hired out, except the children too young for hire. Besides having his food, clothing, and doctor's expenses to meet, he had to pay the very kind widow $12.50 per month, and head-tax to the State of twenty-five cents per month. It so happened that Richard, at this time, was involved in a matrimonial affair. Contrary to the laws of North Carolina, he had lately married a free girl, which was an indictable offence, and for which the penalty was then in soak for him, said penalty to consist of thirty-nine lashes and imprisonment at the discretion of the Judge.

So Abram and Richard put their heads together, and resolved to try the U. G. R. R. They concluded that liberty was worth dying for, and that it was their duty to strike for freedom, even if it should cost their lives. The next thing needed was information about the U. G. R. R. Before a great while the captain of a schooner turned up, from Wilmington, Delaware. Learning that his voyage extended to Philadelphia, they sought to find out whether this captain was true to freedom. To ascertain this fact required no little address. It had to be done in such a way that even the captain would not really understand what they were up to, should he be found untrue. In this instance, however, he was the right man in the right place, and very well understood his business. Abram and Richard made arrangements with him to bring them away. They learned when the vessel would start, and that she was loaded with tar, rosin, and spirits of turpentine, amongst which the captain was to secrete them. But here came the difficulty. In order that slaves might not be secreted in vessels, the slaveholders of North Carolina had procured the enactment of a law requiring all vessels coming North to be smoked. To escape this dilemma, the inventive genius of Abram and Richard soon devised a safeguard against the smoke. This safeguard consisted in silk oil-cloth shrouds, made large, with drawing-strings, which, when pulled over their heads, might be drawn very tightly around their waists. Whilst the process of smoking might be in operation, a bladder of water and towels were provided— the latter to be wet and held to their nostrils, should there be need. In this manner they had determined to struggle against death for liberty.

The hour approached for being at the wharf. At the appointed time they were on hand, ready to go on the boat. The captain secreted them, according to agreement. They were ready to run the risk of being smoked to death; but, as good luck would have it, the law was not carried into effect in this instance, so that the smell of the smoke was not upon them. The effect of the turpentine, however, of the nature of which they were totally ignorant, was worse, if possible, than the smoke would have been; the blood was literally drawn from them at every pore in frightful quantities; but, as heroes of the bravest type, they resolved to continue steadfast as long as a pulse continued to beat, and thus they finally conquered.

The invigorating northern air and the kind treatment of the Vigilance Committee acted like a charm upon them, and they improved very rapidly from their exhaustive and heavy loss of blood. Desiring to retain some memorial of them, a member of the committee begged one of their silk shrouds, and likewise procured an artist to take the photograph of one of them, which keepsake has been valued very highly. In the regular order the wants of Abram and Richard were duly met by the committee, financially and otherwise, and they were forwarded to Canada.

TWO FEMALES FROM MARYLAND—
ANN JOHNSON AND LAVINA WOOLFLEY.

As the way of travel by the U. G. R. R., under the most favorable circumstances, even for the sterner sex, was hard enough to test the strongest nerves and to try the faith of the bravest of the brave, every woman that won her freedom by this perilous undertaking deserves commemoration. It is, therefore, a pleasure to thus transfer from the Old Record Book the names of Ann Johnson and Lavina Woolfley, who fled from Maryland in 1857. Their lives, however, had not been in any way very remarkable. Ann was tall, and of a dark chestnut color, with an intelligent countenance, and about twenty-four years of age. She had filled various situations as a slave. Sometimes she was required to serve in the kitchen, at other times she was required to toil in the field with the plow, hoe, and the like.

Samuel Harrington, of Cambridge District, Maryland, was the name of the man for whose benefit Ann labored during her young days. She had no hesitation in saying that he was a very ill-natured man. He, however, was a member of the old-time Methodist Church. In slave property he had invested only to the extent of five or six head. About three years previous to Ann's escape, one of her brothers fled and went to Canada. This circumstance so enraged the owner, that he declared he would sell all he owned. Accordingly, Ann was soon put on the auction block, and was bought by a man who went by the name of William Moore. Moore was a married man, who, with his wife, was addicted to intemperance and carousing. Ann found that she had simply got out of the fire into the frying-pan. She was really at a loss to tell when her lot was the hardest, whether under the rum-drinker or the old-time Methodist. In this state of mind, she decided to leave all and go to Canada, the refuge for the fleeing bondman. Lavina, Ann's companion, was the wife of James Woolfley; she and her husband set out, together with six others, and were of the party of eight who were betrayed into Dover Jail, and after fighting their way out of the jail, they separated, for prudential reasons. The husband of Lavina, immediately after the conflict at the jail, passed on to Canada, leaving his wife under the protection of friends. Since that time several months had elapsed, but of each other nothing had been known, before she received information on her arrival at Philadelphia. The committee were glad to inform her that her husband had safely passed on to Canada, and that she would be aided on also, where they could enjoy freedom in a free country.

WILLIAM AND ELLEN CRAFT.

A quarter of a century ago, William and Ellen Craft were slaves in the State of Georgia. With them, as with thousands of others, the desire to be free was very strong. For this jewel they were willing to make any sacrifice, or to endure any amount of suffering. In this state of mind, they commenced planning. After thinking of various ways that might be tried, it occurred to William and Ellen that one might act the part of master and the other the part of servant. Ellen being very fair, enough so to pass for white, of necessity would have to be transformed into a young planter, for the time being. All that was needed, however, to make this important change was, that she should be dressed elegantly in a fashionable suit of male attire, and have her hair cut in the style usually worn by young planters. Her profusion of dark hair offered a fine opportunity for the change. So far, this plan looked very tempting, but it occurred to them that Ellen was beardless. After some mature reflection, they came to the conclusion that this difficulty could be very readily obviated by having the face muffled up, as though the young planter was suffering badly with the face or toothache. Thus they got rid of this trouble straightway. Upon further reflection, several other serious difficulties stared them in the face. For instance, in traveling, they knew that they would be under the necessity of stopping repeatedly at hotels, and that the custom of registering would have to be conformed to, unless some very good excuse could be given for not doing so. Here they again thought much over the matter, and wisely concluded that the young man had better assume the attitude of a gentleman very much indisposed. He must have his right arm placed carefully in a sling; that would be sufficient excuse for not registering; then he must be a little lame, with a nice cane in this left hand. He must have large green spectacles over his eyes, and withal he must be very hard of hearing, and dependent on his faithful servant, as was no uncommon thing with slaveholders. To look after all his wants, William was just the man to act his part. To begin with, he was very likely looking, smart, active, and exceedingly attentive to his young master. Indeed, he was almost eyes, ears, hands and feet for him. William knew that this would please the slaveholders. The young planter would have nothing to do but hold himself subject to his ailments and put on a bold superiority. He was not to deign to notice anybody. If, while traveling, gentlemen, either politely or rudely, should venture to scrape acquaintance with the young planter, in his deafness he was to remain mute. The servant was to explain, in every instance, when this occurred, as it actually did.

The servant was equal to the emergency, none dreaming of the disguise in which the Underground Railroad passengers were traveling. They stopped at a first-class hotel in Charleston, where the young planter and his body-servant were treated as the house was wont to treat the chivalry. They stopped at a similar hotel in Richmond, and with like results. They knew that they must pass through Baltimore, but they did not know the obstacles that they would have to surmount in the Monumental City. They proceeded to the depot in the usual manner, and the servant asked for tickets for his master and self. Of course the master could have a ticket, "but bonds will have to be entered before you can get a ticket," said the ticket-master. "It is the rule of this office to require bonds for all negroes applying for tickets to go North, and none but gentlemen of well-known responsibility will be taken," further explained the ticket-master. The servant replied that he knew nothing about that; that he was simply traveling with his young master to take care of him, he being in a very delicate state of health, so much so that fears were entertained that he might not be able to hold out to reach Philadelphia, where he was hastening for medical treatment; and ended his reply by saying, "My master can't be detained." Without further parley the ticket-master very obligingly waived the old rule, and furnished the requisite tickets. The mountain being thus removed, the young planter and his faithful servant were safely in the cars for the City of Brotherly Love. Scarcely had they arrived on free soil, when the rheumatism departed, the right arm was unslung, the toothache was gone, the beardless face was unmuffled, the deaf heard and spoke, the blind saw, and the lame leaped as a hart, and, in the presence of a few astonished friends of the slave, the facts of this unparalleled Underground Railroad feat was fully established by the most unquestionable evidence.

The constant strain and pressure on Ellen's nerves, however, had tried her severely, so much so, that for days afterwards she was physically very much prostrated, although joy and gladness beamed from her eyes, which spoke inexpressible delight. Never can the writer forget the impressions made by their arrival. Even now, after a lapse of nearly twenty-five years, it is easy to picture them in a private room, surrounded by a few friends. Ellen, in her fine suit of black, with her cloak and high-heeled boots, looking in every respect like a young gentleman. In an hour after, having dropped her male attire and assumed the habiliments of her sex, the feminine only was visible in every line and feature of her structure. Her husband, William, was thoroughly colored, but was a man of marked natural abilities, of good manners, and full of pluck, and possessed of perceptive faculties very large.

It was necessary, however, in those days, that they should seek a permanent residence, where their freedom would be more secure than in Philadelphia. Therefore, they were advised to go to headquarters, directly, to Boston. There they would be safe, it was supposed, as it had then been about a generation since a fugitive had been taken back from the old Bay State, and through the incessant labors of William Lloyd Garrison, the great pioneer, and his faithful coadjutors, it was conceded that another fugitive slave case could never be tolerated on the free soil of Massachusetts. So to Boston they went. On arriving, the warm hearts of abolitionists welcomed them heartily, and greeted them and cheered them, without let or hindrance. They did not pretend to keep their coming a secret, or to hide it under a bushel. The story of their escape was heralded, broadcast, over the country, North and South, and, indeed, over the civilized world. For two years or more not the slightest fear was entertained that they were not just as safe in Boston as if they had gone to Canada, but the day the Fugitive Bill passed, even the bravest abolitionists began to fear that a fugitive slave was no longer safe under the stars and stripes, North and South, and William and Ellen Craft were liable to be captured at any moment, by Georgia slave-hunters. Many abolitionists counseled resistance to the death, at all hazards. Instead of running to Canada, fugitives generally armed themselves, and thus said, "Give me liberty or give me death."

William and Ellen Craft believed that it was their duty, as citizens of Massachusetts, to observe a more legal and civilized mode of conforming to the marriage rite than had been permitted them in slavery, and as Theodore Parker had shown himself a very warm friend of theirs, they agreed to have their wedding over again, according to the laws of a free State. After performing the ceremony, the renowned and fearless advocate of equal rights, Theodore Parker, presented William with a revolver and a dirk-knife, counseling him to use them manfully in defense of his wife and himself, if ever an attempt should be made by his owners, or anybody else, to re-enslave them. But notwithstanding all the published declarations made by abolitionists and fugitives to the effect that slaveholders and slave-catchers in visiting Massachusetts in pursuit of their runaway slaves, would be met by just such weapons as Theodore Parker presented William with, to the surprise of all Boston, the owners of William and Ellen actually had the effrontery to attempt their recapture under the Fugitive Slave Law. How it was done, and the results, are taken from the old *Liberator*, William Lloyd Garrison's organ. We copy as follows:

SLAVE-HUNTERS IN BOSTON.—Our city, for a week past, has been thrown into a state of intense excitement by the appearance of two prowling villains, named Hughes and Knight, from Macon, Georgia, for the purpose of seizing William and Ellen Craft, under the infernal Fugitive Slave Bill, and carrying them back to the hell of slavery. Since the days of '76 there has not been such a popular demonstration on the side of human freedom in this region.

The humane and patriotic contagion has infected all classes. Scarcely any other subject has been talked about in the streets or in the social circle. On Thursday of last week warrants for the arrest of William and Ellen were issued by Judge Levi Woodbury, but no officer has yet been found ready or bold enough to serve them. In the meantime, the Vigilance Committee appointed at the Fanueil Hall meeting has not been idle. Their number has been increased to upwards of a hundred good men and true, including some thirty or forty members of the bar, and they have been in constant session, devising every legal method to baffle the pursuing bloodhounds, and relieve the city of their hateful presence. On Saturday placards were posted up in all directions, announcing the arrival of these slave-hunters, and describing their persons. On the same day Hughes and Knight were arrested, on a charge of slander against William and Ellen Craft, the *Chronotype* says, the damage being laid at $10,000. Bail was demanded in the same sum and promptly furnished—by whom is the question. An immense crowd was assembled in front of the Sheriff's office. While the bail matter was being arranged, the reporters were not admitted. It was only known that

Watson Freeman, who once declared his readiness to hang any number of negroes remarkably cheap, came in, saying that that arrest was a sham, all a humbug—the trick of the damned abolitionists, and proclaimed his readiness to stand bail. John H. Pearsons was also sent for and came. The same John H. Pearsons, merchant and Southern Packet agent, who immortalized himself by sending back, on the 10th of September, 1846, in the bark Niagara, a poor fugitive slave, who came secreted in the brig Ottoman, from New Orleans, being himself judge, jury, and executioner, to consign a fellow-being to a life of bondage, in obedience to the law of a slave State, and in violation of the law of his own. This same John H. Pearsons, not contented with his previous infamy, was on hand. There is a story that the slave-hunters have been his table-guests also, and whether he bailed them or not we don't know. What we know is, that soon after Pearsons came out from the back room, where he and Knight and the Sheriff had been closeted, the Sheriff said that Knight was bailed. He would not say by whom. Knight, being looked after, was not to be found. He had slipped out through a back door, and thus cheated the crowd of the pleasure of greeting him, possibly with that rough-and-ready affection which Barclay's brewers bestowed on Haynau. The escape was very fortunate, every way. Hughes and Knight have since been twice arrested and put under bonds of $10,000, making thirty thousand in all, charged with conspiracy to kidnap and abduct William and Ellen Craft, a peaceable citizen of Massachusetts, etc. Bail was entered by Hamilton Willis, of Willis & Co., State street, and Patrick Riley, United States Deputy Marshal. The following is a *verbatim et literatim* copy of the letter sent by Knight to Craft, to entice him to the United States Hotel, in order to kidnap him. It shows that the schoolmaster owes Knight more service and labor than it is possible for Craft to pay:

BOSTON, OCTOBER 22, 1850, 11 O'CLOCK, P.M.
William Craft:

Sir—I have to leave so early in the morning that I could not call according to promise, so if you want me to carry a letter home with me, you must bring it to the United States Hotel to-morrow, and leave it in box 44, or come yourself to-morrow evening after tea, and bring it. Let me know if you come yourself by sending a note to box 44, U.S. Hotel, so that I may know whether to wait after tea or not, by the bearer, If your wife wants to see me you could bring her with you if you come yourself.   John Knight.

P.S. I shall leave for home early on Thursday morning.   J. K.

At a meeting of colored people held in Belknap Street Church, on Friday evening, the following resolutions were unanimously adopted.

Resolved. That God willed us free, man willed us slaves. We will as God wills. God's will be done.

Resolved. That our oft-repeated determination to resist oppression is the same now as ever, and we pledge ourselves, at all hazards, to resist unto death any attempt upon our liberties.

Resolved. That as South Carolina seizes and imprisons colored seamen from the North, under the plea that it is to prevent insurrection and rebellion among her colored population, the authorities of this State and City, in particular, be requested to lay hold of, and put in prison immediately, any and all fugitive slave-hunters who may be found among us, upon the same ground and for similar reasons.

Spirited addresses of a most emphatic type were made by Messrs. Remond of Salem; Roberts, Nell, Allen, of Boston, and Davis of Plymouth. Individuals and highly respectable committees of gentlemen have repeatedly waited upon these Georgia miscreants to persuade them to make a speedy departure from the city. After promising to do so, and repeatedly falsifying their word, it is said that they left on Wednesday afternoon, in the express train for New York. And thus, says the *Chronotype*, they have gone off with their ears full of fleas, to fire the solemn word for the dissolution of the Union.

Telegraphic intelligence is received that President Fillmore has announced his determination to sustain the Fugitive Slave Bill, at all hazards. Let him try. The fugitives, as well as the colored people generally, seem determined to carry out the spirit of the resolutions, to their fullest extent.

Ellen first received information that the slave-hunters from Georgia were after her, through Mrs. George Hilliard of Boston, who had been a good friend to her, from the day of her arrival from slavery. How Mrs.

Hilliard obtained the information the impression is made on Ellen, and where she was secreted. The following extract of a letter written by Mrs. Hilliard, touching the memorable event, will be found deeply interesting:

In regard to William and Ellen Craft, it is true that we received her at our house, when the first warrant, under the Act of eighteen hundred and forty, was issued.

Dr. Bowditch called upon us to say, that the warrant must be for William and Ellen, as they were the only fugitives here, known to have come from Georgia, and the Doctor asked what we could do. I went to the house of the Rev. F. S. Gray, on Mount Vernon street, where Ellen was working with Miss Dean, an upholsteress, a friend of ours, who had told us she would teach Ellen her trade. I proposed to Ellen to come, and do some work for me. Intending not to alarm her, my manner, which I supposed to be indifferent and calm, betrayed me, and she threw herself into my arms, sobbing and weeping. She, however, recovered her composure as soon as we reached the street, and was very firm ever after.

My husband wished her, by all means, to be brought to our house, and remain under his protection, saying: "I am perfectly willing to meet the penalty, should she be found here, but will never give her up." The penalty, you remember, was six months' imprisonment and a thousand dollars fine. William Craft went, after a time, to Lewis Hayden.

He was, at first, as Dr. Bowditch told us, barricaded in his shop on Cambridge street. I saw him there and he said, "Ellen must not be left at your house." "Why, William," said I, "do you think we would give her up?" "Never," said he, "but Mr. Hilliard is not only our friend but he is a U.S. Commissioner, and should Ellen be found in his house, he must resign his office, as well as incur the penalty of the law, and I will not subject a friend to such a punishment for the sake of our safety." Was not this noble, when you think how small was the penalty that any one could receive for aiding slaves to escape, compared to the fate which threatened them in case they were recaptured? William made the same objection to having his wife taken to Mr. Ellis Gray Loring, he also being a friend and a Commissioner.

This deed of humanity and Christian charity is worthy to be commemorated, and classed with the act of the good Samaritan, as the same spirit is shown in both cases. Often was Mrs. Hilliard's house an asylum for fugitive slaves.

After the hunters had left the city in dismay, and the storm of excitement had partially subsided, the friends of William and Ellen concluded that they had better seek a country where they would not be in daily fear of slave-catchers, backed by the government of the United States. They were, therefore, advised to go to Great Britain.

Outfits were liberally provided for them, passages procured, and they took their departure for a habitation in a foreign land. Much might be told concerning the warm reception they met with from the friends of humanity on every hand, during a stay in England of nearly a score of years, but we feel obliged to make the following extract suffice:

> *Extract of a letter from Wm. Farmer, Esq., of London,*
> *to Wm. Lloyd Garrison.*

Fortunately we have, at the present moment, in the British Metropolis, some specimens of what were once American chattels personal, in the persons of William and Ellen Craft and William W. Brown, and their friends resolved that they should be exhibited under the world's huge glass case, in order that the world might form its opinion of the alleged mental inferiority of the African race and their fitness or unfitness for freedom. A small company of anti-slavery friends were accordingly formed to accompany the fugitives through the Exhibition. Mr. and Mrs. Estlin, of Bristol, and a lady friend, Mr. and Mrs. Webb, of Dublin, and a son and daughter, Mr. McDonnell, Mr. Thompson, Mrs. Thompson, Miss A. Thompson, and the Crafts and Brown proceeded to the Exhibition.

BARNABY GRIGBY, ALIAS JOHN BOYES, AND MARY ELIZABETH HIS WIFE, FRANK WANZER, ALIAS ROBERT SCOTT, AND EMILY FOSTER, ALIAS ANN WOOD.

All these persons journeyed from Loudoun county, Virginia, on horse-back and carriage, for more than one hundred miles, availing themselves of a holiday and their masters' horses and carriage. They as deliberately started for Canada as though they had never been taught that it was their duty, as servants, to obey their masters; in this particular, showing a most utter disregard of the interests of their kind-hearted and indulgent owners. They left home on Monday, Christmas Eve, 1855, under the leadership of Frank Wanzer, and arrived in Columbia the following Wednesday, at one o'clock. As wilfully as they had thus made their way along, they had not found it smooth sailing, by any means. The biting frost and snow rendered their travel anything but agreeable. Nor did they escape the gnawings of hunger, traveling day and night, and whilst these articles were in the very act of running away with themselves and their kind masters' best horses and carriage, when about one hundred miles from home, in the neighborhood of Cheat river, Maryland, they were attacked by six white men and a boy, who, doubtless supposing that their intentions were of a wicked and unlawful character, felt it to be their duty, in kindness to their masters, if not to the travelers, to demand of them an account of themselves. In other words, their assailants positively commanded the fugitives to show what right they possessed to be found in a condition so unwarranted.

The spokesman among the fugitives, affecting no ordinary amount of dignity, told their opponents that no gentleman would interfere with persons riding along civilly, not allowing it to be supposed that they were slaves, of course.

These gentlemen, however, were not willing to accept this account of the travelers, as their very decided steps indicated. Having the law on their side, they were for compelling the fugitives to surrender, without further parley.

At this juncture, the fugitives, verily believing that the time had arrived for the practical use of their pistols and dirks, pulled them out of their concealment, the young women as well as the men, and declared they would not be taken. One of the white men raised his gun, pointing the muzzle directly towards one of the young women, with the threat that he would shoot, etc. "Shoot, shoot, shoot!" she exclaimed, with a double-barreled pistol in one hand and a long dirk-knife in the other, utterly unterrified and fully ready for a death-struggle. The male leader of the fugitives, by this time, had pulled back the hammers of his pistols, and was about to fire. Their adversaries, seeing the weapons and the unflinching determination on the part of the runaways to stand their ground, spill blood, kill or die rather than be taken, very prudently sidled over to the other side of the road, leaving four of the victors to travel on their way. At this moment, the four in the carriage lost sight of the two on horseback. Soon after the separation they heard firing, but what the result was they knew not. They were fearful, however, that their companions had been captured.

A paragraph from a Southern paper leaves no room to doubt as to the fate of the two: "Six fugitive slaves from Virginia were arrested at the Maryland line near Hood's Mill, on Christmas Day, but, after a severe fight, four of them escaped, and have not been heard from since. They came from Loudoun and Fauquier Counties."

Though the four who were successful saw no severe fight, it is not unreasonable to suppose that there was a fight, but not till after the number of the fugitives had been reduced to two instead of six. As chivalrous as slave-holders and slave-catchers were, they knew the value of their precious lives, and the fearful risk of attempting a capture when the numbers were equal. The party in the carriage, after the conflict, went on their way rejoicing.

The young men, one cold night, when they were compelled to take rest in the woods and snow, in vain strove to keep the feet of their female companions from freezing, by laying on them, but the frost was merciless, and bit them severely, as their feet plainly showed.

The following disjointed report was cut from the Frederick, Md., *Examiner*, soon after the occurrence:

"Six slaves, four men and two women, fugitives from Virginia, having with them two spring wagons and four horses, came to Hood's Mill, on the Baltimore and Ohio Railroad, near the dividing line between Frederick and Carroll counties, on Christmas Day. After feeding their animals, one of them told a Mr. Dixon whence they came. Believing them to be fugitives, he spread the alarm, and some eight or ten persons gathered around to arrest them, but the negroes, drawing revolvers and bowie knives, kept their assailants at bay, until five of the parties succeeded in escaping in one of the wagons, and, as the last one jumped on a horse to flee, he was fired on, the load taking effect in the small of the back. The prisoner says he belongs to Charles W. Simpson, of Fauquier county, Va., and ran away with the others the preceding evening."

This report from the *Examiner*, while it is not wholly correct, evidently relates to the fugitives above described. Why the reporters made such glaring mistakes may be accounted for on the ground that the bold stand made by the fugitives was so bewildering and alarming that the assailants were not in a condition to make correct statements. We give it for what it is worth.

STOCKHOLDERS IN THE U. G. R. R.

I will give you the names of a few wealthy stockholders of the Anglo-Saxon race:

A. C. Walton, of Lancaster County, Pennsylvania.
Daniel Gibbons,   ''   ''   ''
Michael Whitson,   ''   ''   ''
Thad. Stevens,   ''   ''   ''
Wm. Rickstraw,   ''   ''   ''
Clarkson Browsier,   ''   ''   ''
Lucretia Mott, Philadelphia.
Mayland Brosier, Chester, Penn'a, who has a son, Mayland Brosier, Jr., who is a Senator at the present time.
John Broomer, of Chester County, Penn'a.
Edward Brosier, of Court Square, Chester County.
Horace Greeley, of New York.

Let me give you a few names of the African stockholders:
Raf. Gillmer, of Lancaster City, Penn'a.
Wm. Smith, of Chester   ''   ''
Chas. Martin, of Lancaster   ''   ''
Nelson Wiggins, of New Garden.
Dr. Barrs, of Philadelphia.
Jacobs Gibbs, of Baltimore.
John Brown, of Virginia.
Dr. McEwen Smith, of New York.
George Williams, of Little Briton.

A FEW ITEMS ON SPIRITUALISM.

Now, I am going to give you a few items on Spiritualism. I have heard, from the age of a boy up to the present time, that when a man died he had the power to return to this world in the form of a spirit. I deny it. I am surprised that such intelligent people will keep up such a belief, and instil it in the minds of the youth, in these enlightened times. What! tell me that a man has power to come back into this world in the form of a spirit? Don't believe it. There are but the two places, *Hell* or Heaven, when a man dies, and when his soul goes to Heaven, he don't want to go back, and when he gets to Hell, the *Devil* gets hold of him, and he has no chance to get back again. Yes, writer, but did you not hear, at the time that Christ was crucified, that the dead saints got up and walked on the earth? Ah, reader, is anything impossible for

God to do? That was God's doing. He had power to raise his own life and power to lay it down, and power to raise the dead saints at His crucifixion. My humble belief is, that God is a Spirit, and without him there is no other spirit that has power to visit the earth. Yes, says one, we have mediums who have power to raise the spirits. Those mediums are nothing but sleight-of-hand work and electricity. It causes the table to rock. Until they raise a spirit and bring it before me, I, the writer of this book, will not believe it; and I advise others not to believe it. Let me tell you about a ghost story. A certain man used to gather hickory nuts, and store them away in his loft, and would give them to nobody. When they asked him for some, he said, "No. What I can't eat, I want the people to put the remaining in my grave." So when he died they did so. So two men concluded to go and steal sheep one night. One of them had some hickory nuts and a hammer in his pocket. Going through the woods, he came across this graveyard, and sitting down on the tombstone, began to crack his hickory nuts, and said to his partner, "I will stay here and keep watch, while you go down and see where the sheep are." In the meantime a carpenter came by, who lived not far from the graveyard. He came unto his partner very much alarmed, saying, "I have heard very much about the old man cracking hickory nuts, but to-night I saw it with my own eyes;" and his partner, who was sick with the rheumatism for a long time, answered, "I won't believe it unless I see it with my own eyes." He said, "Just get on my back, and I will carry you out there and show him to you." As they were going along by some bushes, he said, "Don't you hear him?" "Yes, but I want to see him. Take me a little further." And he carried him along until he got within sight of him, and said, "Don't you see him?" And the man who was sitting there, cracking hickory nuts, thought it was his partner with the sheep, and they stood still looking at him, and he says, "Is he fat? Is he fat? *I say, is he fat?*" And the fellow that had him on his back give him a chuck, and says, "Here he is, take him, fat or lean!" and the ghost broke and run, and the other man run, and the lame man beat his partner home. So much for that ghost story. So you see, reader, ghosts and spirits are nothing but imagination. The only spirit we have is Alcohol, and when it gets into a man it stretches him out, and sometimes persons come along and imagine it is a ghost. So ends the ghost story and Spiritualism.

ABOUT BIGAMY.

Let me give the reader a few items on Bigamy. They say bigamy is a wrong and a curse to the land. So say I, but I noticed, during my visit to Salt Lake, that it is one of the handsomest cities in the United States, with beautiful streams of clear water running through the streets. And Brigham allowed a man to have as many wives as he was able to take care of, but he must be able to take care of them. There were no whisky-mills, no dance-houses, and no gambling-houses, and no houses of ill-repute. Let us see the difference. Since Americans have been there, there are dance-houses, whiskey-mills, gambling-houses, and houses of ill-repute. Let me ask the reader a question: How is it that in the United States men run away with other men's wives, married men keeping three or four different women, outside of the family circle, and no notice taken of that? Which is the best law, to allow a man to marry a number of women and be able to take care of them, or allow a man to marry one and be not able to take care of her, and running away with several, and no notice of it? Then I am not an advocate of these doctrines, but I only say that we, some of the colored people, who are possessed of little learning, take notice of these matters. Look at Salt Lake four years ago, and look at it to-day, and you will see the difference. I say Brigham is an old man, and I say that we should let him alone during his lifetime.

About the Modoc War.
a few items that came under my notice.—
the great terrific modoc war in oregon.

We, the American Army, have opened fire on this 16th of April, 1873, on the Modocs. And the battle was so great that we had to issue an extra record, telling the people that we have got the favorable position of the Modocs and holding it in possession, and our soldiers are strung along for over a mile on their best battle-ground, and the Warm Spring Indians, about seventy-five, on the other side, leading the way. And we have thrown a few shells into their camp, and there is not an Indian to be seen. And the Warm Spring Indians fought bravely. And the Modocs say they are nearly *hell*. And by to-morrow, which is the 17th, there won't be any Indian left. They will all be killed. But here is the 8th day of May, 1873, and the only account that we have is, that there are only two killed. But they have slaughtered our soldiers too shamefully to record. And sent three of our best men—General Canby, Dr. Thomas, and Colonel Wright—to the grave, by the large band of Modocs, forty-seven *warriors*, while there was from 800 to 900 soldiers and Warm Spring Indians; and the idea of letting the best men be killed! It is a disgrace, according to my belief, to the American Government. The proceeding of such disgraceful acts I will not proceed to record any more.

Precious Scripture Words.

Be ye, therefore, merciful, as your Father is also merciful. Judge not, and ye shall not be judged: condemn not, and ye shall not be condemned: forgive, and ye shall be forgiven.

Give, and it shall be given unto you: good measure, pressed down, and shaken together, and running over, shall men give unto your bosom.

For with the same measure that ye mete withal, it shall be measured to you again. And he spake a parable unto them. Can the blind lead the blind? Shall they not both fall into the ditch? The disciple is not above his master, but every one that is perfect shall be his master. And why beholdest thou the mote that is in thy brother's eye, but perceive not the beam that is in thine own eye? Either how canst thou say to thy brother, Brother, let me pull out the mote in thine eye, when thou thyself beholdest not the beam that is in thine own eye? Thou hypocrite! Cast out first the beam of thine own eye, and then shalt thou see clearly to pull out the mote that is in thy brother's eye. For a good tree bringeth forth not corrupt fruit, neither doth a corrupt tree bring forth good fruit. For every tree is known by its

fruit; for of thorns men do not gather figs, nor of a bramble-bush gather they grapes. A good man out of the good treasure of his heart bringeth forth that which is good, and an evil man out of the evil treasure of his heart bringeth that which is evil; for of the abundance of the heart his mouth speaketh. And why call ye me, Lord, Lord, and do not the things which I say? Whosoever cometh to me, and heareth my sayings and doeth them, I will show you to whom he is like: He is like a man which built a house, and digged deep, and laid the foundation on a rock, and when the flood arose the stream beat vehemently upon that house and could not shake it, for it was founded on a rock. But he that heareth, and doeth not, is like a man that, without a foundation, built a house on the earth, against which the stream did beat vehemently, and immediately it fell, and the ruin of that house was great.

CALIFORNIA.

California as she always was, as she always will be. California not as she was, but as she is at the present time; not as she is at the present time, but as she will be. Writer, how explain this? In early times we had surface diggings, only a foot from the surface of the earth, and every poor man could have a claim of his own. Not so now. We have hydraulic diggings, owned by large capitalists. Then not as she was, but is at the present time. California was always a rich country for gold, and always will

be. Then as she always was so she always will be. Though she was a rich country, we had no large capitalists. Then not as she was. She was not noted then for such respectable societies as she is at the present time. We had no such buildings as Stanford's and Crocker's then as she has at the present time. We had no State Capitol, and railroads running through the State then as she has now. When I came to this State they had neither railroads, steamboats, stages, or carriages. Now, when I look around in San Francisco, I see splendid coaches and carriages. I could not see, at that time, fifty ladies in San Francisco. Now I see Montgomery street thronged with one thousand ladies. In my humble belief Montgomery and Kearny streets, in San Francisco, excel Chestnut street, in Philadelphia. Then California, not as she was, but as she is at the present time. Not as she is at the present time, but as she will be. We now cultivate our own soil, and raise our own provisions. We don't need to send East for provisions any more, as we did in early times. She does not support her ownself, but she supports other countries. Then may the writer say: as she always was, so she always will be. These things which I have recorded have come under my notice since I arrived in California, in 1851.

This book was commenced in 1869, and printed in 1873. I, James Williams, commenced to sell pamphlets of my book in April, 1853. The only fault I have with California is, that there is not Christianity enough. Though we have large churches, in my belief there is but little religion. I believe California is one of the most ungodly sections of the United States. Reprint April, 1893.

THE CHINESE IN CALIFORNIA.

I now proceed to record a few items about the history of the Chinese in California. I believe, giving a rough guess, there is about 70,000 Chinese in California. And all appear to be industrious and persevering in business, and prosperous, own a large amount of property in the cities of San Francisco, Sacramento, and other places, and large store establishments. Some of our true Americans say they don't want them here; that they will get so numerous that we Americans can't live. Didn't God create the Chinaman as well as the American? He never made a mouth but that He prepared bread to fill it. Then let us trust in Him, and He will prepare ways for us all, and take care of us all likewise. What would we do in the State of California but for the Chinamen? The rich people couldn't get along without them; for servants and cooks, whether white or colored, it is difficult to hire; therefore, they must have Chinamen as house servants. But, they say, we must drive the

Chinamen out of California, for they work so cheap. As cheap as they work, they pay more for rent, and are taxed more than any other race of people. Drive them out? Ah, my learned friends, are you not aware that California is a free country? It is a part of the United States of America, and America throws open her doors for all nations. Now let me tell you a tale that I have heard from the age of a boy to the present time. In New York City, and the City of Philadelphia, in 1844, 1845, a cry was raised among the true American people against the Irish people. Allow me to use the phrase that the people used at that time. Some would say, "the Irish," others would say, "The damned Irish are all immigrating here from Ireland; that we, the American people, would be starved, and couldn't get work on account of the Irish." But take notice, please, that the Irish have lived, we have lived, and no one has been starved yet.

I want to call your attention to the fact, that in 1855, in Sacramento, there was a bill introduced into the Legislature to prohibit colored men from immigrating to the State of California, and that those that were here should leave, and those that did not leave should be taxed heavily, and should wear tags; also, the same law was introduced in Oregon. While this was going on, Great Britain threw open her doors and invited us to Vancouver's Island. We commenced to flock there like bees, and the Sacramento merchants and property-holders began to intercede, and the bill went under the table, and we are all living in harmony up to the present time, and nobody is hurt yet. So, you see, my winning friends, that the Irish and the Niggers have outlived that sentiment, and now it is the Chinamen. Who are the best workmen we have in America? The Irish. Who build your railroads? The Irish. Who run your locomotives? The Irish. Who build your canals? The Irish. Who fought your battles in the war? The Irish. Who work your hydraulic diggings in California? The Irish. Who increased the value of property in San Francisco? The Irish. While the true Americans, white and black, would come and look at the sandhills, would stick their hands in their pockets, and would walk away and say, "I wouldn't give two cents for the whole place." But the Irishman would come along, and squat his little tent, and would say, "This place will be good sometime," and he continued to improve it, day after day, until his place became quite valuable. Then the American, like the eagle on some tall tree, watching the fish-hawk until he caught a fish, became anxious for the place, though he toiled none. If he couldn't buy at his own figure, he would set up some scheme or other to rob him out of it by bogus titles. So you will see what these three classes had to undergo.

OPINIONS OF THE PRESS.

The *Evening Torchlight*, of Oakland, says, that James Williams, once a slave in Maryland, has written in pamphlet form a history of his life and adventures. It sets forth many strange and adventurous tales, interesting and amusing. He canvassed Marysville and Sacramento, and sold many copies in both places. He is now selling his book in Oakland, and we can assure our readers that it is well worth the price asked for it. The Sacramento *Bee* says, that James Williams, once a fugitive slave, has written an interesting book, containing a great amount of interesting and amusing matter, and is well worth the price asked for it. It reminds us of Defoe's "Robinson Crusoe" and "Sinbad the Sailor." A library, whether private or public, is not complete without one of these books. The Stockton *Evening Herald* says: This afternoon there was laid on our table a pamphlet, entitled "Life and Adventures of James Williams, a Fugitive Slave, with a full description of the Underground Railroad." The work is an entertaining one, and those who have hitherto doubted the imaginative powers of this persecuted race should read it and disabuse their minds. The California San Francisco *Alta* says, that James Williams, a fugitive from slavery, has written a book of his experience, detailing the manner of operating the Underground Railroad. The author, who is an undoubted African, is offering his work for sale in person, and gives some interesting reminiscences while talking with his patrons. The Virginia *Chronicle* says, that James Williams, a fugitive slave, has laid on our table a book, containing an account of his many adventures and escapes from slavery, and a full description of the Underground Railroad. From a hasty glance through the book we incline to the opinion that it is an interesting one, and is worth the price asked for it. We hope that the citizens will patronize and aid him in selling his book. The Gold Hill *Evening News* says, that James Williams, a colored man, is canvassing Gold Hill for the sale of a book, comprising his life and adventures while a slave at the South, his escape from slavery, a full description of the famous Underground Railroad, whereby said escape was effected, and other good reading matter. It is a neatly printed pamphlet of over 100 pages, and well worth reading.

CHARLES A. RUSSELL.

Reader, I will now record a few facts about the execution of Charles A. Russell, who was executed at San Francisco, Friday, July 25, 1873. These facts came under my notice, therefore I record them. He suffered the death penalty in the County Jail Yard, about half-past two, for the murder of James Crotty. He and his victim had been drinking through the day, and both got quarrelsome. They had an altercation on the streets during the day, but were parted before they came to blows.

Russell, a few hours later, met his victim in Cady's saloon, on the southeast corner of California and Montgomery streets, and the quarrel was renewed, Russell reminding Crotty that he had arrested him in Salt Lake for robbery, while occupying the position of U.S. Marshal, and Crotty retorting that he had never been in the State Prison, as Russell had. They finally came to blows, but again were separated by friends, and Russell left, vowing vengeance against his adversary. He went to several places to borrow a pistol, but failing in that, he went and bought one, and had it loaded. In passing Cady's saloon, he saw Crotty standing at the bar taking a drink. He stopped, and taking his pistol from his pocket, he cocked it, and advancing towards Crotty, who was unconscious of his presence, placed his hand on his shoulder, and as Crotty turned around, fired the pistol in his face. The bullet tore away a portion of the face and passed through his head, inflicting a ghastly wound, of which he died in a few days. He, Russell, was tried in the 15th District Court, on 9th of January. He was defended by H. P. Barber and A. M. Crane, but the testimony was conclusive, and he was convicted of murder in the first degree, and sentenced by Judge Dwinelle to be hung on the 21st of March. A motion was made for a new trial, but it was denied. The Supreme Court, after examining the case, found nothing to warrant them in granting a new trial, and the judgment of the lower court was affirmed by Judge Dwinelle, who, on the 27th of May, re-sentenced Russell to be hung on the 25th of July, 1873. The time passed quickly by to the doomed man, and to his many friends, who were using

every endeavor to have the sentence commuted. He was attended by the
Rev. Doctors Dodge, Cunningham and Williams, of the Presbyterian
Church, in which faith he was educated. He was also attended by Dr.
Carpenter, who remained with him up to ten o'clock of the night before
the execution. In the meantime, the scaffold was being erected; it was
the same on which Devine was hung. Shortly after five o'clock, Russell
awoke from his sleep. After making his toilet, he spent an hour with
the ladies in religious devotions. At half-past ten o'clock, Russell was
removed from his cell to the one next to the scaffold. He was neatly
attired in a black suit, which he wore at the trial. Here he remained in
conversation with Drs. Cunningham, Carpenter, and Dodge. At twelve
o'clock the prison door was opened to admit those who had invitations
from the Sheriff to witness the execution, and in a few moments several
hundred people were inside the gates. In the meantime, Russell's friends
were trying to obtain a commutation of sentence from the Governor.
The execution was to take place at one o'clock. At a few minutes past
one, a dispatch was received, granting a respite of ninety minutes.

The Reverend Doctors, in the meantime, had sent dispatches to
Governor Booth to obtain a pardon, who was at Donner Lake. The
landlord of the hotel telegraphed back that the Governor was out with
a boating party, and that the message could not reach him before three
o'clock. The jailer having received this news, reported it to the Sheriff,
who reported it to the prisoner, and told him that no reprieve had been
granted, and that it was time for him to prepare. At a few minutes
past two, Sheriff Adams emerged from the cell, followed by Russell. He
walked up the steps leading to the scaffold with a steady step. He took
his place on the trap, and standing erect and firm, he cast an undaunted
look on the crowd below him. He trembled with nervous excitement,
and the muscles of his face twitched convulsively.

A prayer was offered up by Dr. Carpenter in his behalf. The black
cap was then drawn over his head, but was immediately raised by Dr.
Carpenter, who said, "Kiss me good-bye, Charles." The Doctor stepped
back, the signal was given by the Sheriff, the trap fell, and the doomed
man was left hanging between heaven and earth. The body swung
rapidly around several times, but there was no struggle, not a muscle
moved, and there was no visible sign of life. After hanging for about

thirty minutes, he was examined by the doctors, he pronounced life extinct; he was immediately cut down and placed in a fine coffin, upon which was a silver plate, bearing the following inscription, "Charles A. Russell. died July 25, 1873."

His Career.

He was born in the City of New York—where his parents now reside—in August, 1843, and therefore was thirty years of age. At an early age he left school and went to learn the printer's trade. He was intelligent and ambitious, and applied himself diligently to his case and study, until he became master of the trade, and acquired a fair education. When the Civil War broke out and the President issued the first call for volunteers, Russell abandoned his case in the office of *Frank Leslie's Weekly*, and entered the army. He was a brave soldier, and did good service for his country. He served his term of enlistment, and was honorably discharged. For three years after his discharge he led an idle and dissolute life. In 1867, he came to this coast, in search of his brother Phillip; but when Charles arrived here, he found out that his brother had enlisted and gone to Arizona. He soon found himself without money or friends, and resorting to his modes in the East, he was soon spotted by the police. A short time afterwards he was arrested for stealing a suit of clothes in Sacramento, tried, and was convicted, and sentenced to the State Prison for three years. After his discharge from the State Prison, he went to Utah, and obtained a position as U. S. Marshal, and there made the acquaintance of Crotty, the man whom he murdered. He afterwards came to this State, and worked as a waiter in a restaurant in Sacramento City. He afterwards went to Vallejo, and there worked in a restaurant for Mr. Page. In the course of time, Page saw indications of criminal intimacy between his wife and Russell. A quarrel ensued, and Russell came to San Francisco, and became involved in the quarrel which led to his death. Page and his wife quarreled and separated, in consequence of her conduct with Russell. The latter wrote several letters to Mrs. Page while in jail last summer. Page intercepted two of them, and published them, as proofs of his wife's infidelity and Russell's bad character. Page was arrested and tried for tampering with the mails. While the trial was pending, he shot his wife, and, supposing that he had killed her, blew his brains out. Mrs. Page recovered and visited Russell frequently while in jail, until Russell's friends, who were striving to have the sentence commuted, intimated to her that her visits would not help his case any, and she discontinued them. Russell denies the charge of intimacy with her, and that, with the statement that he did not intend to kill Crotty, constitute the main points in the statement to Dr. Carpenter, the truth of which he solemnly affirmed on the gallows, just before being launched into eternity.

I, the writer of this book, record his history that it may be an example to the rising generation.

Young men, shun drink and all vices, and you will not fall into this corral; for drink is the cause of Russell being led to the gallows. Oh! young ladies, as you read this book, take warning likewise, and may God help you to shun it also.

THE MODOCS.

I, the writer, record the hanging of the first Indians in the United States of America. Captain Jack, Sconchin, Black Jim and Boston Charley, Modocs, were hung October 3, 1873. Where they got the law from to hang the first Indians in the United States of America I do not know. Whether Congress has passed an Act authorizing State or Territory to hang Indians, or imprison them for life, I do not know. My opinion is, that the lower class of the Anglo-Saxon race have driven the Modocs into this horrible crime which they have committed, by the unjust ways in which they have dealt with them. I have traveled this part of the country for more or less than twenty-four years, among the Indians, and I have never been molested by them. I have also visited the camps by myself, been in the caves with them, and witnessed the war-dance, and never was molested yet. Reader, I believe that they were trying to

deal with Captain Jack like they deal with the freedmen down South, but Jack didn't see the point; they used to send out agents to collect money for the freedmen and distressed soldiers during the war, and they would stick the money in their pockets; they would also bring great donations of clothing and provisions to them from different parts of the Northern States; and what did they do with them? They could not pocket that, but they made an auction, and sold them to the highest bidder, and those poor freedmen, who could not buy at auction, had to take a spin around the block and go without. Said the agents, "This had to be done to pay expenses." That was a plan they took to pocket more money. If this is a lie, I am not to be blamed, for the freedmen told me so down South. This is what they were playing on Captain Jack, but he would not stand it, and you hung him. I say it was wrong to hang him, because there was no law established by Congress to hang him. Let me hold Jeff Davis before you, reader, and ask you what you think of him? He was the cause of thousands of lives being lost, and widows distressed to-day in our land; cause of our President of the United States being assassinated. Was there no law to hang Jeff Davis, according to Congress? I say there was. Then why didn't you do it? If he had been a poor Indian, we would. Remember, my reader, God created the Indian, the same as any American.

Jack and his followers were hung at Fort Klamath, California, October 3, 1873. Slolux and Barancho were pardoned. The gallows was erected by Hiram Fields, post carpenter.

The last day on earth of the savages was distinguished by a big talk, which lasted five hours. Dave Hill, one of the head men of the Klamath tribe, and Oliver Applegate, acted as interpreters.

The Chaplain opened the talk. The Indians all listened attentively. Sconchin and Jack were the most attentive. The sentence was then read to them. Jack then replied: "I have heard the sentence, and know what it is; but I feel I am more innocent than Hooka Jim, Bogus Charley, and Steamboat Frank. These young men started the murder. I was always in favor of peace. Bogus Charley was the first to propose the murder of General Canby. When Bogus proposed it, Boston sanctioned it. Bogus said, 'If you fail to help me, I will do it myself.' I know that Shacknasty killed Canby and shot Meacham, and Boston killed Thomas."

Speeches were then made by the savages, but, of course, to no advantage. Captain Jack then referred to what Boston had said about his share in the massacre, and remarked: "Scarfaced Charley is my relative. He is a worse man than I am. I would like to make friends with General Wheaton, and punish the right parties." This caused great amusement, much to the disgust of the chief. He concluded: "If I am to die, it is well. I am ready to go and see my Great Spirit above."

Sconchin then spoke as follows: "You all know me; I was always a good man; there never was a time that I did not want a white man's heart and ask advice from white men. I sent my boy to Yainox Reservation, and he chose a piece of land for his home. Boston Charley told the truth when he called me a woman. I was like a woman, and my voice was against war. I was always a peace man, but there was some young men that were rash and anxious to distinguish themselves. Hooka Jim and some other boys made the trouble, and when I look at the irons on my legs, I feel as though they ought to wear them. I have always given the young men advice, shook hands with the whites, and here I

am now, condemned, with irons on my feet. I heard what the Great
Spirit man had to say, and I think it good. I should not die for what
others have done, but I will not find fault with the decision, but will
go to meet my father in the Spirit-land. My own father lived and died
long ago, when I was a boy. I often thought I should like to go and
meet him in the brighter world, with the Great Spirit. If the law kills
me and I go up to the Spirit-land, perhaps the Great Spirit will say to
me, 'Sconchin, my law has taken your life, and I accept of you as one
of my people.' It was not in my heart to do wrong; but I was led away
by the wishes of the young people. You know whether I am good or
not, for you have tried the law on me. Hooka Jim always thought he
was strong, a good shot, and did these things contrary to my wish. I
spoke against the murder of the Commissioner. When the Big Chief in
Washington read the evidence all over, he must have been led to believe
that Sconchin was wicked savage, and did not know that Sconchin had
used all his influence with the young men to keep them from doing
these rash acts. The Great Chief has to depend on the evidence which he
gets from his subordinates, and perhaps thinks Sconchin a bad, wicked
man, while Sconchin has been a good, quiet Indian all the time. I will
try to believe that the President is doing according to the will of the
Great Spirit in condemning me to die. You may all look at me, and see
that I am firm and resolute. I am to die. I leave my son. I hope he will
be allowed to remain in this country. I hope he will be a good man.
I have always looked on the younger men of my tribe as my especial
charge, and have reasoned with them, and now I am to die for their
bad character. I leave four children, and I wish them turned over to
my brother Yainox. It is doing a great wrong to take my life. I would
like to see those executed for whom I am wearing chains. I do not
say my sentence is not right; but after our retreat from Lost River, I
thought I would come in and surrender myself. I felt that the boys had
committed the murders, and that I had been carried along with the
current. If I had blood on my hands, like Boston Charley, I could say,
like him, I killed Canby—I killed Thomas. But I have nothing to say
about the decision, and I never would ask it to be crossed. You are the
law-giving party. You say I must die. I am satisfied if the law is correct.
I have made a great speech. I would like to see the Big Chief, face to

face, and to talk with him, but he is a long way off, like at the top of a mountain, while me at the bottom, and cannot go to him. My heart tells me that I should not die—that you do me a great wrong in taking my life. War is a terrible thing. All must suffer—the best horses, the best cattle, and the best men. I can now say let Sconchin die." The Chaplain now offered up an eloquent prayer. The venerable man wept like a child at its conclusion. The squaws and children of the old man were taken in the guard-house to take a last farewell. The anguish of the women was frightful. Scarfaced Charley, Hooka Jim, and Bogus Charley refused to see the condemned, and asked to be placed where they could see the execution. Six graves were dug a short distance from the post guard-house. Some one offered $2,000 for Jack's body.

The Morning of the Execution.

The prisoners were led out, and seated in a wagon. The column then marched to the place of execution. The four condemned Indians were conducted to the drop, and the ropes adjusted by Corporal Ross, of Company G, Twelfth Infantry. Jack was placed on the right, next Sconchin, then Black Jim and Boston Charley. After adjusting the ropes, the Post-Adjutant read the orders of the President in regard to the execution of the sentence. Scarfaced Charley, Shacknasty Jim, and Bogus Charley enjoyed the liberty of the camp. Scarface was liberated because the military recognized in him the best and fairest warrior in the tribe, and the one at present exerting the greatest influence over the band. He had no share in the Canby massacre, and though he is reputed to have killed more soldiers than any other Indian, he killed them all in open, square warfare. He was in no way concerned in the murders on Lost River, though he fired the first gun of the war.

SOME ANTECEDENTS OF THE MODOC WAR.

The Modocs are a part of a race whose career has been marked with bloody deeds. They are an offshoot of the Klamaths. It was during a revolution that the race became dismembered, and one Modoc broke off and established an independent race. Jack was the first chief among them worthy of note. His explanation of the matter is, that some white men, while passing through the country, had their horses stolen, and therefore opened war on the Modocs. This happened in 1864. Seventy-five emigrants were killed, and many more were laid away in Oregon. At this time, Ben. Wright was elected Captain of an independent Company in Yreka, and proceeded to the Modoc country on a mission of vengeance. He first tried poison and failed; he then had a peace talk. The Indians came, laid down their bows and arrows; and, on a given signal being made by Wright, forty were killed; a treaty was then made by Steele, and in the same year another was made by Huntington, which proposed that the Modocs should take up their residence on the Reservation. They did so, but soon returned to the old quarters. In 1859, Meacham was appointed Superintendent, but failed to conciliate them. They refused to return to their new homes, and Jack treated with insult the overtures made to him. He finally resolved to go to the Klamath Reservation, on condition that he should be allowed to select his home. At this point, the Medicine Man arose to his feet, and said, "We won't go there," drawing a pistol while speaking. A discussion then ensued, and the result was that the Modocs were allowed till next morning to consider. Jack then returned to camp, at which time a proposition was made to assassinate Meacham. In the meantime, peace was being tried to be made, and Commissioners were sent out for that purpose. The first Commission consisted of Meacham, Applegate, and Samuel Case, and was sent out to consult with Captain Jack, but, fearing treachery, he would not come out. On the 4th of March, Steele and Riddle were sent out to the Modocs, to explain the terms of peace more fully. He found that the Indians had washed off the white paint of peace, and were preparing for hostilities. The talk between them and the Indians was stormy. Jack said that the country was his, and he would fight before being moved; that he would not meet the Commissioners. On the 6th, the Indians seemed to relent. They sent word by a squaw that they accepted the terms of peace offered by Steele.

On the 9th, wagons were sent out to meet the expected Modocs, but none came, and the wagons returned empty. The second Commission was now composed of Dr. Thomas, Dyer, Applegate, Steele and Meacham. On the 6th of April, arrangements were made to meet the

Indians on the 8th. Both sides were fearing treachery, and consequently the meeting was deferred from day to day. On setting out for the place, Toby Riddle held my horse, says Meacham, and told me not to go. A consultation was held, and it was resolved to meet the Indians. On reaching the ground, the party found Captain Jack and six of his men. Before dismounting, I was satisfied that the Indians were all armed with revolvers, and this put me on the severest trial of my life. How the first moments were passed I hardly know. It was only in manoeuvering for positions, the Indians making numerous changes, in order to bring the Commission party near together, and as far from them as possible. In that they were successful, though Dyer and myself were working to prevent it. Canby and Thomas did not seem to understand it. Hooka Jim went to my horse, and secured him with a sage-brush. Then he put on my coat, and this confirmed my belief that treachery was to be enacted. Canby then made a short speech, and then turned and asked Thomas to speak. He made his speech coolly and calmly, with that slow distinct manner so peculiar to him. Sconchin then made a short speech, and, while Riddle was interpreting, there was seen coming from ambush two warriors, each with an armful of guns. The party arose to their feet, and I asked Jack what this meant. He replied by pulling a pistol from his side, and crying out that all was ready, at the same instant pulling the trigger of his pistol. The cap exploded, but the charge did not. He raised his pistol the second time and fired, the ball striking the general in the face. He then retreated a distance of forty yards, followed by Jack, and finally fell on the rocks, and then Jack stabbed him in the neck, and Ellen's man shot him with a rifle. Black Jim was to have dispatched Dyer, but he was not in position, and Jack ordered Hooka Jim to shoot him. Hooka Jim followed him for several hundred yards, but did not catch him. Sconchin was to have been my slayer, and he approached me with a revolver and knife. His first shot grazed my left shoulder. In return I aimed at Sconchin's heart, but it failed to fire. I then ran, pursued by Sconchin, who fired, shooting me in the arm. Some of these shots stunned me, and I became unconscious. Boston Charley then prepared to take my scalp, but Toby interposed, with devices, to delay operation, and when at length he had raised five or six inches of my scalp, Toby shouted, "Soldiers! soldiers!" and Boston left his work unfinished. Returning to consciousness some time after, I heard the word of command given to the soldiers, and I knew I was saved. The war was resumed.

On the 16th of April the attack on the Lava Beds began, and lasted all day, the Indians disputing every inch of ground. On the third day they were thought to have left the Lava Beds and gone southward. On the 26th of April, while Captain Thomas was reconnoitering the Lava Beds, he was surprised, and forty-five of sixty-five men were lost. Soon after, General Gillim was relieved of the command, and General Davis succeeded. The Indians were harassed, shot, and driven by the troops until the 22d of May. Seventy Modocs surrendered, Captain Jack and some warriors still remaining in the field. To assist in his capture, Bogus Charley, Hooka Jim and Shacknasty Jim volunteered. On the 29th Jack and all his warriors surrendered to General Davis. Thus ended the Modoc War.

THE FIRE IN THE YELLOW JACKET MINE, GOLD HILL.

Now, reader, I will record for you some items about the great fire that occurred in Gold Hill, September 21, 1873.

About three o'clock, September 20th, a fire was discovered in the Yellow Jacket Mine, Gold Hill. Soon after the fire was discovered, and while efforts were being made to extinguish it, there occurred a heavy explosion. Not long after the first explosion, a second one occurred of a heavier nature. As soon as the news of the fire reached the surface, the whistles of the works sounded an alarm of fire, and other whistles soon chimed in, bringing out the Gold Hill Fire Department. The origin of the fire seems to be involved in a mystery. Near the Belcher blacksmith shops in a winze, reaching to the 1100-foot level. About eleven o'clock of the night before, some of the timber at the foot of the winze took fire. The blacksmith then on duty extinguished this fire, as he thought, but not being quite sure that it was out, he told Louis Louizelle, who was next on duty, to see that the fire did not again break out. A fatal mistake was in throwing water down the main shaft. When the firemen reached the grounds, a dense volume of smoke was pouring out of the top of the shaft, and, by forcing the water down, forced the escaping gases through the Crown Point. The situation of the men below, down on the 1400 and 1500-foot levels, was most perilous for a time, that is, while the gases were being forced back by the water. One of the men, unused to mines, at the time of the explosion cried out that some one had thrown a stone down the incline, when the others, with ears better educated, cried out that some accident had happened above. All at once hastened up the incline, and reached the surface in safety. All the lights not blown out by the first were extinguished by the second. The fiery blast injured Albert Lackey, Albert Burt, and Jacob Laity. Lackey's hair and whiskers were nearly burned off, and his clothing much burnt. The hoisting of the men was performed with safety and precision. The cages were rushed up and down the shafts, with their living freight, at a terrific rate of speed.

List of the Killed.—George B. Mudd. He was a native of Missouri, and was forty-two years of age. He left a wife and four children. He was a member of Clifton Lodge, No. 16, F. and A. M. His funeral took place under the auspices of the Masonic fraternity. James Waters, carman, at the Crown Point, was also found suffocated on the 1100-foot level of the same mine. He lived but a short time after being brought to the surface. He was a native of County Roscommon, Ireland, and was thirty five years of age. He had a father, mother, and sister, residing at Lowell, Massachusetts, from a visit to whom he had lately returned. James Niles was also found on the 1100-foot level of the Crown Point. He was overtaken and overpowered by the gas while engaged in eating his supper. He was highly esteemed, was a native of Kennebec county, Maine, and was forty-two years of age. He left a wife and six children, from whom he had been separated for ten years. Louis Louizelle was an underground blacksmith, in the employ of the Belcher Company. His body was found about 200 feet from the blacksmith shop, where the fire first started. He was a native of St. Mary's, Lower Canada, aged forty-four years. He left a wife and three daughters. W. S. Broadwater was a carman, and his body was found near the Jacket switch. He was unmarried, a native of Missouri, aged fifty years. He was a member of the Sarsfield Guard and Gold Hill Miners' Union. Thomas Cusick worked in the Crown Point. He was a native of County Limerick, Ireland, age twenty-eight years, and was a member of the Gold Hill Miners' Union. He has a sister in Wisconsin. He was unmarried.

The Injured.—Albert Lackey, underground foreman of the Belcher, was badly burned while in the mines, trying to save his men, and is badly poisoned by the gas. Jacob Laity, another underground foreman, was brought to the surface in an insensible condition, but will recover. He worked like a hero in the lower levels. Albert Bevet, an underground foreman, was also raised to the surface in an insensible condition. He had grasped the cross-bar of the cage with such a grip that it required the strength of two men to loosen his hold when he arrived at the surface. William Jones, foreman of Liberty Engine Company, No. 1, was badly asphyxiated. William Pritchard, of the Crown Point, while attempting to escape from the mine, had his hair badly singed and his eyebrows burned off. James Dixon, John Shannon, John Young, and John Hays, cut and bruised. There were sad scenes about the works of the Yellow Jacket and Crown Point Mines, and while the fire was still raging, and explosions taking place under the ground, the excitement was intense. Hundreds were soon collected about the hoisting works, as the majority of these had friends and relatives in the fiery lower levels. When the dead and dying were brought to the surface, and the worst fears of some were realized, some heart-rending scenes were enacted. There were also joyful meetings and greetings. Efforts to confine the fire were made as soon as it was possible to enter the mines in safety, which was shortly after the last explosion. Sam Jones, Superintendent of the Crown Point, at once set men to work at closing all communication between his mine and the Jacket. The timbers were knocked out of the drifts for the space of several feet, and the points so cleared filled with dirt. In the direction of the Imperial and the Old Yellow Jacket works the same precautionary measures were adopted.

It was determined to give the fire no chance to spread, though it was luckily in a place where there was little danger of its extending to other sections of even the Yellow Jacket. The fire was soon discovered to be in the winze, extending up from the 1300-foot level to the 1100-foot level, and to this winze it had been confined. The fire burned the timbers out of the winze between the two levels named. The Gold Hill firemen were early on hand and had worked like heroes, though their efforts at first were misdirected. But as soon as they were directed, they were actively engaged everywhere. Some of the Virginia firemen were actively engaged. Luckily there was an abundance of water in the tanks connected with the works, hydrants near at hand, and plenty of hose. Men got down in the mines, and, carrying strings of hose through the 1100-foot level, attacked the 1100-foot level. A hole was cut in the pump-column and hose attached at a point where, by properly working the pump, a pressure of 200 feet of water was obtained. In the start, men took the Babcock fire-extinguishers, kept in the mine, and, approaching near, played upon the fire at the bottom of the winze. Little could thus be done, as the burning brands and timbers dropped down the winze faster than any could be extinguished. It required two or three days for the timbers to burn out of the winze.

Rats Asphyxiated.

Throughout the levels of the mines, where the poisonous gas and flames swept, were to be seen, lying upon the floor, hundreds of rats. They were probably startled from their hiding-places by the explosion, or came out upon the floors when they found it difficult to breathe in their holes. At any rate, they came out and were killed in great numbers. Where a rat cannot exist, how could man be expected to live? The dead human bodies were carried to an undertaker's, as soon as taken out of the mines. A large crowd was collected about the undertaker's nearly all day, viewing the bodies. Coroner Holmes, who was just from California, impanelled a jury, and held an inquest on the bodies of the victims of the disaster, on Tuesday afternoon, at ten o'clock, at the office of Justice Wright, Gold Hill.

Some Further Particulars About the Washoe Mines, &C.

Now, reader, I will proceed to inscribe the names of the principal mines, and describe their hoisting works, also the location of the ledge of the honey-combed city, which is called Virginia City. Why do you call it the honey-combed city? Because she is tumbled all over—all through full of holes, like a honey-comb. Sierra Nevada, Gold & Curry, Savage, Hale & Norcross, Chollar Potosi, Julia, Imperial and Empire, Gold Hill Quartz, French, Bacon, Eclipse, Jacket, Crown Point, Belcher, Seg. Belcher, Caledonia, Knickerbocker, Baltimore, Overman, Silver Hill, Kentuck, Dayton, Arizona, Utah. All those mines are extensive mines, and have extensive hoisting works also. This visit I paid there in 1873. These hoisting works have also powerful machinery, and large and powerful walking beams. The depths of these mines are 1400 feet, 1500 feet, 1600 feet; the furthest depth, according to my knowledge, is 1700 feet, but they run down a perpendicular so many feet, then glance off to an incline. The cage is double-decked, carrying down twelve men at a time, six men in each cage; and in each tunnel four men to a pick. One works about ten minutes, he falls back to take air, and another takes his place, and so it continues until they go round. They work eight hours, at four dollars a day. Those tunnels are about five to six feet wide, and six feet high. As they work, they lay a floor and side-up and cap overhead, to secure against the falling of the dirt, and they lay their railroad track on the floor. They work three or four feet ahead of them, and throw the dirt in the cart, and run it out of the tunnel on to the hoisting works. Many places where the rock is stout, they tunnel for hundreds of feet without casing, and throw the dirt behind them. In the mines, tunnels are crossing each other, running east and west, north and south. That is what we call the honey-combed city. They can go from one company's mine to another. A man who is unacquainted with these mines would lose himself, and could not find his way out. The silver ledge commences at what is called the Old Comstock, and runs north and south.

During my visits there, in 1873, I discovered that the ledge laid in pillars. You will find it in one place, then, for 200 or 300 feet, you will find it again; then it disappears for 200 or 300 feet—then you will find it again. This is what I mean by saying that it lies in pillars. I came to a conclusion, and do believe, that these mines are the richest in the world. There is more money in that city, and more in circulation there than any other city on the Pacific coast. I then took a full observation from Gold Hill and Silver City, which extends about five miles from Virginia City. Gold Hill and Silver City are about one-fourth of a mile wide, and thinly settled. I also noticed that Carson Valley is a beautiful valley, and plenty of farming seemed to be done at this time. I also noticed that Jack's Valley is a beautiful valley, and plenty of farming to be done at this time. I noticed that Carson City is thriving rapidly. They have built a beautiful mint, which is in operation; also, a State

Capitol, which is the Capitol of the State of Nevada. Reader, you need
not think that these items are fictions, for I have crossed the summit of
the Sierra Nevada seventeen times, four times on foot, and made safe
journeys. Thank God for so much. Let me give you a few items how the
people get wood off the highest mountains in Washoe Valley and Carson
Valley. In some places they build a long trough, carry the wood there, put
it in, then it runs to the foot of the mountain, and they then put it in cars.

In other places they build flumes, and carry it round the mountains,
just as they want it, for four and five miles, or further. Upon the tops
of these mountains there are lakes; they carry the water from the lakes
to these flumes, and they put on a big head of water in these flumes
from the lakes. Then they throw the wood in, and the force of the water
carries the wood down to a trussel-work, which is built on the level of

the surface of the earth; there they have men to take it out of the water and throw it on the ground, and there they have cars to load it in, and carry it into the city. I noticed, in 1873, in crossing over the C. P. R. R., that they have snow-sheds forty-five miles long, large and extensive wooden pillars, a foot and a half thick, so if the cars should run off the track, they could not run off the grade. I hear a great deal about the railroad, but I think they deserve a great deal of credit for building such a road; but it seems like they get no credit. My opinion is that fifty miles of that C. P. R. R. cost more than all the U. P. put together, or any other road in the United States.

I now conclude this book, and promise to give you more at some future time. The following piece is clipped from the Yolo *Democrat*:

We have been presented by the author with a copy of a work just published by himself, being an account of his own life and adventures, entitled "Life and Adventures of James Williams, a fugitive slave, with a full description of the Underground Railroad." Williams is a very pleasant, intelligent colored man, who has lived on this coast many years. He was formerly a slave in Maryland, but escaped under an assumed name. We have not had time to examine the work critically, but, from a cursory glance, judge it to be well gotten up, and liberal in its ideas towards other races, particularly the whites. He will remain in town a day or two, and call upon our people, so that they can, for fifty cents, procure a copy of his book, and help a poor man—Twenty-four Years of Life and Adventures in the State of California.

Let us rejoice and sing unto the Lord God of hosts.

There is a fountain filled with blood
    Drawn from Emanuel's veins,
And sinners plunged beneath that flood
    Are losing all their guilty stains.

      Chorus—I do believe, I now believe
           That Jesus died for me,
           And by his blood, his precious blood,
           I shall from sin be free.

Thou dying Lamb, thy precious blood
    Shall never lose its power,
Till all the ransomed church of God
    Be saved, to sin no more.

      Chorus—I do believe, I now believe, etc.

THE CHRISTIAN'S VOYAGE THROUGH LIFE AND DEATH.

Though the sea is rough and stormy,
And the winds blow fierce and loud,
Jesus Christ shall be my captain
And I'll make the port at last.

Chorus—We're out on the ocean sailing,
      Homeward Bound we swiftly glide;
      We're out on the ocean sailing
      To a home beyond the tide

Jordan's billows all around me,
And the stormy tempests rage;
Jesus shall command the ocean,
And will give a homeward breeze.

Chorus—We're out on the ocean sailing, etc.

Yes, I think I see the city,
And the light-house on the shore;
Hark! I hear the angels singing,
Come, oh come, my brother, come!

Chorus—We're out on the ocean sailing, etc.

Yonder comes the angel pilot,
Comes to waft my spirit home;
Soon with them I shall be singing
There with Moses and the Lamb.

Chorus—We're out on the ocean sailing, etc.

Soon I shall be in the Kingdom,
Soon I shall outlive the storm;
Soon I shall be in the Kingdom,
There around my Father's throne.

Chorus—We're out on the ocean sailing, etc.

There the winds will all be silent,
There the tempest never rage,
All the sailors that are faithful
There shall meet to part no more.

Chorus—We're out on the ocean sailing, etc.

There I shall meet my brother,
I shall meet my father, too,
And with them I shall be happy,
And never, never part again.

Chorus—We're out on the ocean sailing, etc.

Index